Jean McMann

Riddles
of the
Stone Age

Rock Carvings of
Ancient Europe

with 153 illustrations

Thames and Hudson

Half-title page: *Detail of an upright,
Table des Marchands, Locmariaquer,
France. Cf. 74–75.*

Title-page: *Carved boulder, Fuente de
la Zarza, La Palma, Canary Islands.*

Contents: *Triple spiral in the chamber
at Newgrange, Co. Meath, Ireland.*

Maps drawn by Hanni Bailey

Printed in The Netherlands by Drukkerij de
Lange/van Leer, Deventer and London

Contents

Preface   9

1 The great stones   11

2 Passage-grave art   23

3 Cup-and-ring art   88

4 Maltese ornament   118

5 Antiquarians, archaeologists
and astro-mystics   138

6 Possibilities   146

Notes   154

Acknowledgments   155

Select bibliography   156

Index   157

For my children, Elizabeth and Mark

1 Spirals and basin stone in the west recess at Newgrange.

2 Drilled ornament, Mnajdra, Malta.

Preface

This book is a beginning rather than a culmination for me and, I hope, for its readers. Its purpose is to introduce the abstract inscriptions carved in stone in Atlantic Europe, northern Italy and Malta during the Neolithic period.

Seeking out and photographing these symbols and then labouring and rejoicing (and at times despairing) over the pictures in my darkroom has given me an intuitive appreciation of them. I have traced the designs (some are very difficult to draw) in order to know them kinaesthetically. I have pinned them to my wall, so that I can see them every day. I have tried to make a direct connection with them which bypasses dictionary definitions and scientific data. Photographs have been an invaluable means of approaching the symbols directly, and the photographs are the essence of the book.

Although I feel that I 'know' the symbols, in perhaps the same way I might say I knew a good friend, I find it difficult to define them or tell you exactly what they are. Archaeologists and historians have furnished valuable information, intuition has brought me closer to them, and yet I continue to look for other avenues of approach, such as the study of the human mind. This book represents the first step in what I hope will be a journey of discovery for author and reader alike.

Distribution of megaliths

N

ORKNEY

NORWAY

SWEDEN

NORTH

SEA

UNITED
Achnabreck

REPUBLIC
OF
IRELAND
Newgrange
Bryn
Celli Dau

Ilkley Moor

DENMARK

KINGDOM

NETHER-
LANDS

WEST EAST

POLAND

R.Elbe

Avebury
Stonehenge

BELGIUM

GERMANY

R.Oder

ATLANTIC

GERMANY

CZECHOSLOVAKIA

BRITTANY
Carnac

R.Seine

R.Rhine

R.Danube

OCEAN

R.Loire

FRANCE

SWITZER-
LAND

AUSTRIA

HUN-
GARY

Valcamonica

R.Po

YUGOSLAVIA

PORTUGAL

R.Ebro

R.Tagus

SPAIN

La Granja de Toniñuelos
Dolmen de Soto
R.Guadalquivir
Cueva de Menga
(Antequera)

BALEARIC IS.

CORSICA

ITALY

SARDINIA

MEDITERRANEAN SEA

SICILY

CANARY ISLANDS
LA PALMA

0   Mls   300

0   Km   500

ALGERIA

TUNISIA

MALTA

0   Mls   300

0   Km   500

3 Map of Western Europe showing the principal sites mentioned in the text.

CHAPTER ONE

The great stones

Stone Age people left their mark all over the world. At first they painted about hunting, deep in caves. In France and Spain especially, but also elsewhere in the world, images of animals and hunting rituals are found, still fresh and magnificent although painted as many as fifteen to thirty thousand years before the birth of Christ. They seem to have served as hunting magic, yet the artists show affection for the animals as well as pleasure in the act of painting itself.

It is thought that the cave painters believed they had ancestral connections with the animals; this belief could explain the reverence and affection reflected in their work. Later, the character of the art changed. During the Neolithic, or Late Stone Age (from 5000 to 2000 BC in Europe), the realistic and often light-hearted representations of hunters and animals disappear. The art becomes abstract. Spirals and geometric designs appear on stones and rock surfaces, sometimes executed with great care and finesse, at other times hastily scratched – like a doodle. Many are inscribed on single stones standing or lying in fields, usually near the sea. Others are carved on stone temples and burial structures.

The megaliths, as these monuments are called (from the Greek: *megas*, 'large'; *lithos*, 'a stone'), remain a mystery. They lie scattered across Europe, India, Asia and even America, though no links have been found between these different megalithic regions. The ones that we shall be concerned with in this book occur mainly in Atlantic Europe. Stonehenge, begun before 2500 BC, is the famous example, but megaliths were

being built hundreds of years earlier than this in the British Isles, Scandinavia, Germany, France, Spain, Portugal and Malta. There are a wide variety of surviving monuments. 'Menhirs' (single standing stones) and 'dolmens' (a large 'capstone' supported by three or four other stones, forming a small cist-like space) are the simplest types. Alternatively the giant stones, only roughly shaped into slabs, may make up the walls and roofs of chambers. These are often covered with rubble and earth, creating a cave in which the dead were interred, sometimes generation after generation. Passages leading up to the caves provide the name, 'passage graves'. Other structures consist of stones arranged in circles – for example, 'henge' monuments such as Stonehenge and Avebury – or rows – for example, Carnac in Brittany – both formations that have been linked to astronomy, especially alignments with the sun or moon at certain times of the year. The stone temples of Malta are yet another type of megalithic structure, unique to this island culture.

For many years, archaeologists thought that the skills in building and design manifested by the megalith builders had been imported from more advanced civilizations in the Near East. The oldest stone structures in the world were considered to be the Egyptian pyramids, the oldest temples those in Mesopotamia, so it was logical to assume that megalithic architecture, whether in Malta or Brittany, derived ultimately from the East. The discovery in the late 1940s that certain organic materials could be dated by measuring the amount of radiocarbon they contained did

11
9

5, 10

not at first upset this traditional view. By and large, the new radiocarbon dates seemed to confirm that innovations in architecture and most other aspects of civilization were made earlier in the Orient than elsewhere. It was not until these dates were checked or 'calibrated' against the annual growth rings of 5,000-year-old bristlecone pine trees in California, and found to be as much as 800 years too young before 1200 BC, that a revolution in archaeological thinking came about. For the megaliths were found to be earlier than their supposed sources. The pyramids of Egypt, dated on historical written evidence to 3000 BC and after, could now be seen to be 1000 years *later* than many chamber tombs in Brittany, dated by calibrated radiocarbon to before 4000 BC. Even Britain and Denmark had stone tombs by 3300 BC, while the Maltese temples, begun soon after, can lay claim to be the world's first free-standing stone structures, as Colin Renfrew (a noted archaeologist concerned with prehistory and dating) has pointed out.[1]

The megaliths, then, show that their builders possessed considerable intelligence and sophistication. Not only do the architectural methods appear to have been originated independently in several different geographical areas, but alignments such as that at Stonehenge show highly developed systems of geometry and astronomy.[2] We are discovering that archaic societies had unsuspected skills and wisdom, and perhaps that is one reason for the renewed interest in prehistory. Anthropologists, neuro-physiologists,

psychologists, architects, artists and even photographers have become fascinated with the megalithic. New theories and observations are springing up in disciplines far from archaeology, and it seems certain that what we know about the Stone Age will become much richer for these ideas.

Why did these early people spend so much time and energy building and ornamenting structures clearly designed for ritual rather than for dwelling places? The presence of human remains together with other clues in the European megaliths implies that their function had to do with ideas about death – that they were constructed out of love or fear of the 'ghosts' or souls of departed ancestors. Other sites, such as those in Malta, show no sign of being built for burial. The absence of extensive grave-goods, such as those found with buried royalty in Egypt, leaves us with a scarcity of clues. There are, however, in many of the megalithic monuments, cryptic messages from their makers.

These messages are the subject of this book. The abstract symbols carved by human beings in the Late Stone and Early Bronze Ages are found as widely distributed as the megaliths themselves. They form a striking and significant development in prehistoric art. Coming as they do during the period when people began to settle and farm and build and perhaps to become more reflective about life, death and the seasons, they may signal the first attempts of the human race to evolve a written language.

4 Cairn at Nether Largie Farm, Kilmartin, Argyll, Scotland.

5 Altar with drilled ornament, Mnajdra, Malta.

6 Corbelled vault of the chamber, Newgrange, Co. Meath, Ireland.

7 Passage grave, La Roche-aux-Fées, Brittany, France.

8 Uprights lining the passage, Newgrange, Co. Meath, Ireland.

9 *Stone rows at Le Menec, near Carnac, Brittany, France.*

10 Ħaġar Qim, Malta.

11 Part of the Great Circle at Avebury, Wiltshire, England.

12 Standing stones at Temple Wood, near Kilmartin, Argyll, Scotland.

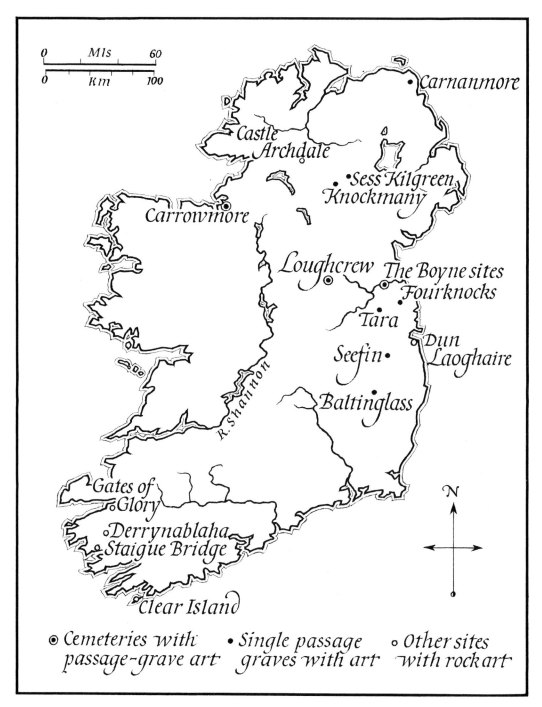

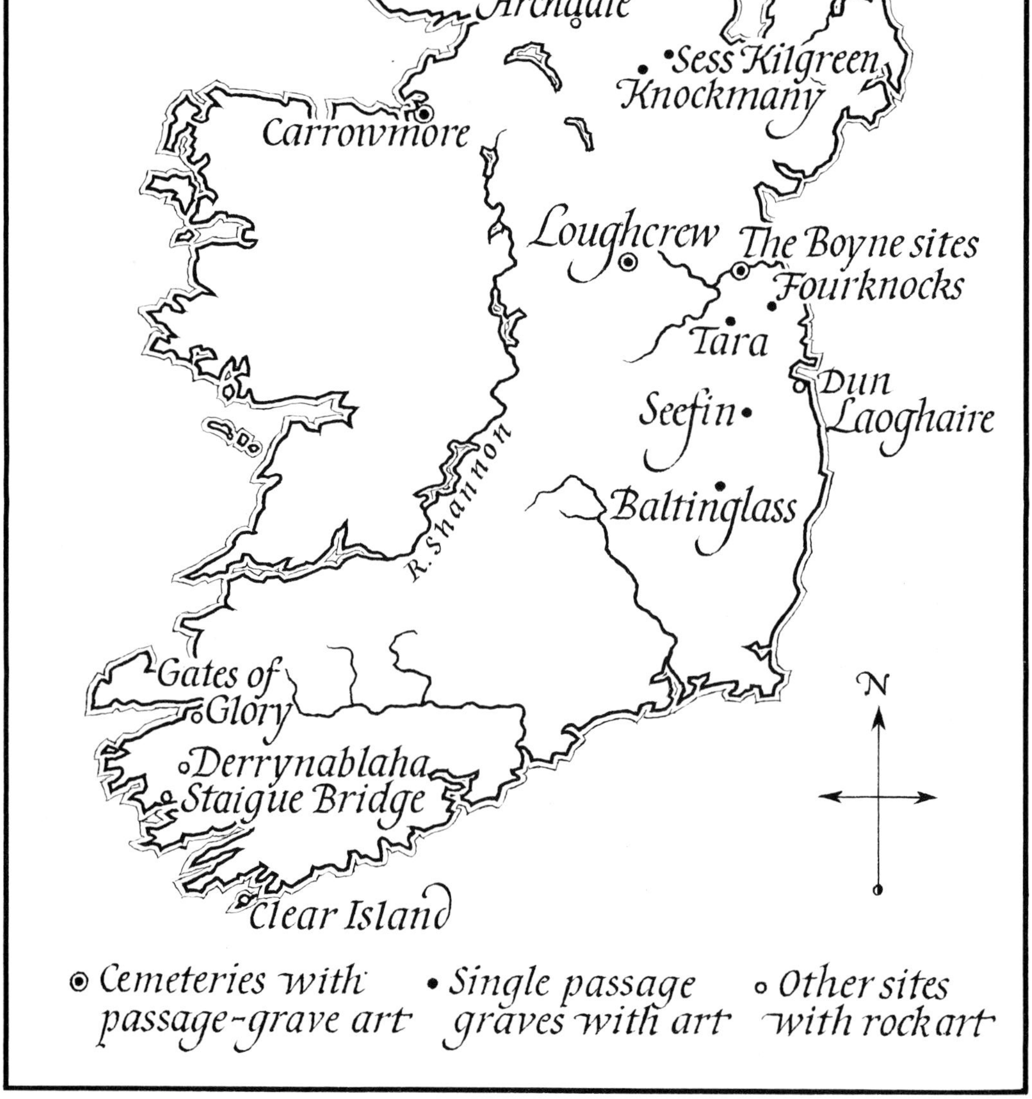
0 Mls 60
0 Km 100
Carnanmore
Castle Archdale
Sess Kilgreen
Knockmany
Carrowmore
Loughcrew
The Boyne sites
Fourknocks
Tara
Dun Laoghaire
Seefin
Baltinglass
R. Shannon
Gates of Glory
Derrynablaha
Staigue Bridge
Clear Island
N
Cemeteries with passage-grave art
Single passage graves with art
Other sites with rock art

13 Map of Ireland, showing relevant sites.

CHAPTER TWO

Passage-grave art

Although Stone Age symbols are widely scattered throughout Atlantic Europe, Italy and Malta, there are intriguing similarities from country to country. One characteristic style is incorporated into the architecture of the great burial chambers, such as the passage graves at Gavrinis in Brittany and Newgrange in Ireland. Another group of symbols, known as cup-and-ring marks, appears almost exclusively on isolated outcrops of rock or on boulders, and occasionally on standing stones, found singly or in alignments. A third category of motifs is found in Malta, carved into the soft workable limestone of the temples there. All three groups are quite distinct, though they share some basic motifs (such as the spiral, which occurs occasionally among the cups and rings and frequently in the other two groups).

The repertoire of passage-grave art consists mostly of joined groups of circles and arcs, lozenges, zigzag, serpentiform and spiral designs.[1] They appear in tombs in western and northern Europe: mainly Ireland, Great Britain, France, Spain and Portugal. Many archaeologists, including the famous Abbé Breuil, an authority on cave art, have argued that the designs are for the most part anthropomorphic – conventionalized representations of the human form. Others, such as the excavator of the Newgrange passage grave, Professor M. J. O'Kelly, and Evan Hadingham, author of a valuable book on the British carvings,[2] warn against seeing human faces and forms where none may have been intended. Indeed, a good deal of imagination would be required to see many of the supposed 'faces' invoked by partisans of the anthropomorphic.

Anthropomorphic or not (and probably not), the finest expression of the passage-grave style is the stone which marks the entrance to Newgrange in Ireland. This great chambered tomb lies in County Meath, about 25 miles north of Dublin, together with two other important passage graves (Knowth and Dowth) and a host of smaller satellite tumuli. Here, the ancient burial mounds nestle in a bend of the River Boyne; Newgrange itself has a fine view across the green valley. In ancient times this was no doubt the cemetery made famous in Irish literature from the 10th century AD onwards as Brugh na Boinne, but known in folklore from much earlier. The kings of Tara may have been buried here, and the ancient god Dagda Mor.

20

Newgrange was then, and remains, a remarkable work of architecture, faced with shining white quartz from the river. The tumulus, according to early sources, was flat-topped, and could be seen for miles. It has been restored by the Irish Public Works Department to what it may have been when it was constructed (some time before 3000 BC). Today, 11 m (36 ft) high, it forms a prominent feature of the landscape, although certainly not so striking as in ancient times, and perhaps a bit too tidy and modern in profile.

19

Around the Newgrange tumulus are placed 97 slabs (in addition to the entrance stone) in a continuous circle. None is quite so fine as the entrance stone, but most are ornamented with the motifs typical of the art of the passage graves: spirals, lozenges, chevrons or zigzags, triangles, and arrangements of parallel lines or arcs. Suns and flower-like designs are found on other tombs in the area.

29

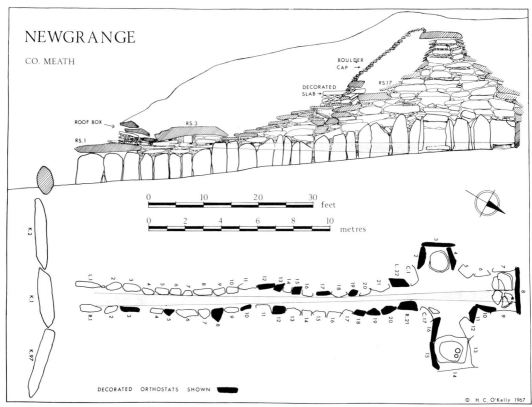

NEWGRANGE

CO. MEATH

14 Sectional elevation and plan of Newgrange, showing the path of
the sun's rays at the midwinter solstice. Courtesy of Prof. M. J. O'Kelly.

The glacial boulder which marks the entrance is of green gritstone, probably quarried within a few miles.[3] About 3.2 m (10 ft 6 in.) long by 1.3 m (4 ft 3 in.) high, it has been carved with spirals and parallel arcs and lozenges (or diamonds) over its entire surface. The symbols are placed with a fine sense of design, deeply and masterfully carved. The surface has been 'pick-dressed' (lightly pocked to remove the glacial patina) so that it is a uniform light green. There is a mysterious vertical groove near the centre of the boulder, occurring also on another kerbstone, and on the entrance stone at nearby Knowth.

The carving techniques are characteristic of the passage-grave artist: flint or quartz points picked out the designs, which were first lightly incised as a guide. Sometimes an area round a design was picked away, forming a relief. Or the entire stone might be pick-dressed after the designs were completed, as was in fact the case at Newgrange.

The carved slab is the most striking feature of the entrance to Newgrange, but there are other elements of interest. A doorstone once fitted into the entry formed by the first pair of orthostats (uprights), framed across the top by a stone lintel. Above this doorway, set back a little into the cairn, is a narrow opening with a lintel carefully carved with lozenges. This slit or fanlight, at present a device unique in the architecture of the

24

tombs, has proved the source of a fascinating phenomenon, as we shall see.

Inside, the passage, 18.9 m (62 ft) long, is lined with orthostats leading to the chamber itself. On the uprights, designs are carved, some well planned and executed, others awkward and revised. There are three niches leading off the chamber, each with a basin-shaped stone. The centre niche, facing back down the passage, has a triple spiral on one of the stones. It is a lovely design, for many years the subject of a tale to the effect that at a certain time of year, the sun came into the chamber and illuminated it. The tales were dismissed by sensible people, of course.

However, on the winter solstice, 21 December 1969, Professor O'Kelly awaited the sunrise inside the passage grave. Here are his notes:

At exactly 09.54 hours BST the top edge of the ball of the sun appeared above the local horizon and at 09.58 hours the first pencil of direct sunlight shone through the roof-box and right along the passage to reach across the tomb chamber floor as far as the front edge of the basin stone in the end-chamber. As the thin line of light widened to a 17 cm band and swung across the chamber floor, the tomb was dramatically illuminated and various details of the side- and end-chambers as well as the corbelled roof could be clearly seen in the light reflected from the floor. At 10.04 hours the 17 cm band of light began to narrow again and at exactly 10.15 hours the direct beam was cut off from the tomb. For 17 minutes, therefore, at sunrise on the shortest day of the year, direct sunlight can enter Newgrange, not through the doorway, but through the specially contrived narrow slit which lies under the roof-box at the outer end of the passage roof.[4]

The chamber at Newgrange represents an extraordinary achievement, both in terms of the elegance of the space inside, and the engineering which permitted it. As the passage widens into the chamber, the height of the orthostats increases a little, and the roof rises to form a bee-hive dome. Between the great slabs of gritstone are layers of smaller stones, crushed by the weight of the slabs and the tumulus, thus forming a level bed for the tremendous weight of the roof.

As a result, only two of the roof stones have broken across in the thousands of years since the tomb's construction.[5]

Decoration in the tomb repeats, for the most part, the themes represented on the entrance stone. The orthostats are pick-dressed to emphasize the patterns; only two have striking ornamentation. One (designated L19 by Claire *28*

15 Midwinter solstice at Newgrange. At dawn on the shortest day of the year, for about quarter of an hour, the sun's rays shine through a slit beneath the roof-box to illuminate the whole passage and rear wall of the chamber.

16 *Mr Michael Smith, the caretaker at Newgrange.*

appear in a number of Irish tombs, was discovered at Knowth. (It is hidden away at present, because of the continuing excavations there.) According to archaeologists, the basins at Newgrange and other tombs, such as Baltinglass, may have been used to receive cremated bones during an interment ceremony. The right-hand (east) recess is most often used and emphasized by decoration or larger size, perhaps indicating an ancient preference for right over left.[6]

The rather meagre finds,[7] or grave-goods, in these tombs give us a few tantalizing clues to the character of the megalith builders. The finds consist of stone and clay balls or 'marbles', pottery, bone pins (perhaps used to fasten clothing, or to close leather bags containing ashes), bone beads and pendants, often made with semi-precious stones, and in the shape of tools. Most of these small items are burnt, suggesting that they were cremated with their possessors.

The ornaments which have been obtained by sifting through the ashes and debris on the floors of these chambers indicate, according to Herity,[8] a sophistication in keeping with the architecture. It is fair, he maintains, to assume (although direct evidence of the clothing itself is lacking) that the attire was as refined as the ornament. Thus, the picture emerges of a folk possessing skills in architecture and engineering, with ceremonies and rituals accompanying cremation of the dead, and a sense of 'personal elegance' in their everyday adornment.

Herity and George Eogan have suggested that a 'priest-architect class' existed even before the Boyne tombs were built, an idea supported by Euan MacKie for the British Isles as a whole.[9] There must have been leadership capable of organizing construction gangs of perhaps a hundred able-bodied workers at one time. Using simple technological resources,[10] such as levers, inclined ramps, sledges, rollers as well as manpower for traction, with ropes of vegetable fibre

O'Kelly, whose guidebook should be consulted by visitors to the monument) shows a bold set of spirals and zigzags. The other, L22, has zigzags of less certainty.

The three recesses, or niches, at the west, north and east of the chamber, remind one of the cruciform plan of Christian churches. Certainly it is an effective space for ritual, the rise of the roof creating a dramatic contrast to the feeling of enclosure in the passage.

There is a basin stone in the west recess, another, broken, in the north recess, and two, one inside the other, in the east recess. The upper one of these last two is carefully shaped out of granite, with two cups sunk near the rim, whereas the other basins are of sandstone and slate. The finest example now known of these basins, which

and rawhide, these people erected the structures which are now regarded as having been the shared cemeteries of the community leaders and their families.

At Knowth, the largest tumulus of the Boyne group, there is a rival to the achievement of the artist and architect at Newgrange. The tomb is under excavation now, as it has been since 1962, and no doubt will be for many years hence. The public is understandably prevented from access during this time, and the art on the kerbstones is hidden beneath sheets of black plastic. The repertoire of symbols is similar to that at Newgrange, but the style of carving is quite different. There is a less dramatic sense of composition; the designs are not so deeply carved, nor do they relate so closely to the form of the boulders. Serpentiform lines and concentric arcs are the most common elements. *32–5*

Knowth, three-quarters of a mile northwest of Newgrange, was at one time probably as much as 11 m (36 ft) high, with as many as 140 kerbstones. Early archaeologists, although they investigated the mound with its 15 satellite graves clustered

17 Map of the Newgrange area.

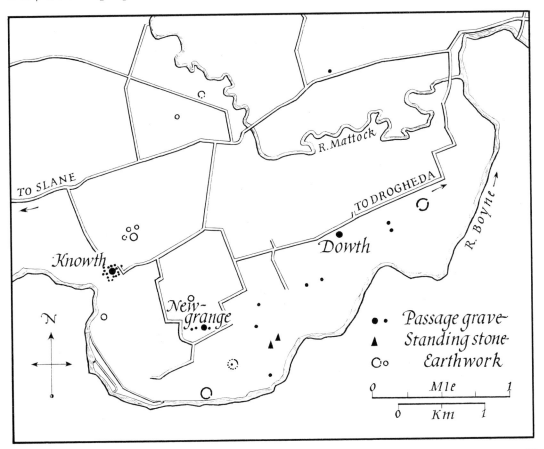

around the base, could not find a main passage. It was not until 1967 that a long passage was discovered, with an entrance stone bearing a vertical groove like that at Newgrange. Inside were decorated stones, and a chamber bearing the same ornament as that at the entry.

Excavators were astonished when in 1968 another equally long passage was discovered. This second passage began opposite the first, running through to a second chamber separated from the other one by only a few metres. Both passages seem to have been built at about the same time. It was inside the second chamber that the carved stone basin was discovered, lying broken in the right recess.

When excavations are completed, so that one can see the entire structure with its kerbstones ranged around it and the cairn with its chambers and magnificent basin, perhaps a proper comparison can be made with the architecture at Newgrange. The style of the art, though closely related, is quite distinct, and it should provide a striking display. Until then, the visitor is well rewarded by visits to Newgrange and Dowth, which are both within walking distance of Knowth.

Dowth, 1¼ miles northeast of Newgrange, is the third of the three major passage graves in the Boyne valley. Here, on one of the kerbstones, you will find one of the most charming and apparently representational symbols in passage-grave art – seven suns, carved and placed on the stone in what seems to be a rather carefree manner. Inside are more decorations, and if you are devoted to such pilgrimages, it is worth submitting to the claustrophobic conditions: descent down a steep iron ladder by flashlight into the damp, murky chamber below, no doubt quite suitable for the dead.

At Loughcrew, about 30 miles west of Dowth, a local schoolmaster, Eugene Alfred Conwell, made an astonishing discovery in 1863. Picnicking with his wife on the Hill of the Witch, he noticed 29 cairns, which proved to be another prehistoric cemetery, or 'necropolis'. In one is a stone basin nearly 2 m (6 ft) across, and on many of the stones·in the chambers are decorations reminiscent of those at Dowth. Rayed, flowery 'suns', concentric arcs, and a folksy, almost comic-book style of carving are characteristic.

The fourth major concentration of passage-grave art in Ireland is not far away, about 10 miles south of the Boyne group, at Fourknocks I. This is, perhaps, after Newgrange, the most impressive architecturally, for the chamber is 4.9–6 m (16–20 ft) in diameter. Upon entering, one is struck immediately by the forceful use of ornamentation. Above two of the three generous recesses are imposing lintels, inscribed with bold zigzags and lozenges. Another, which bears a simpler chevron pattern, is placed above the entry passage. The effect is dramatic and spacious, a masterpiece of the passage-grave style in which architecture and symbolic ornament combine to produce a sacred space worthy of the most significant ritual.

Although there are many other examples of the passage-grave style in Great Britain and Ireland,* the only rival to the architectural and artistic achievements at the Boyne cemeteries and Fourknocks is found on the tiny island of Gavrinis, in France. Here, you must catch the boat from Larmor-Baden, on the Breton coast near Auray, where a sign announces hourly departures from the dock (though beware, for there is no boat in winter).

Once on the island, the mound of Gavrinis is accessible after a short walk uphill. There is a small doorway tucked into the hillside, and the visitor who steps inside is presented at once with an astounding wealth of ornament. Twenty-two of the 29 orthostats comprising the tomb are completely covered with masterly designs. The

---

* For example, in Ireland at Sess Kilgreen, Knockmany, Clear Island, Seefin and elsewhere, at Bryn Celli Ddu and Barclodiad y Gawres in Wales, and the Eday Stone from Orkney.

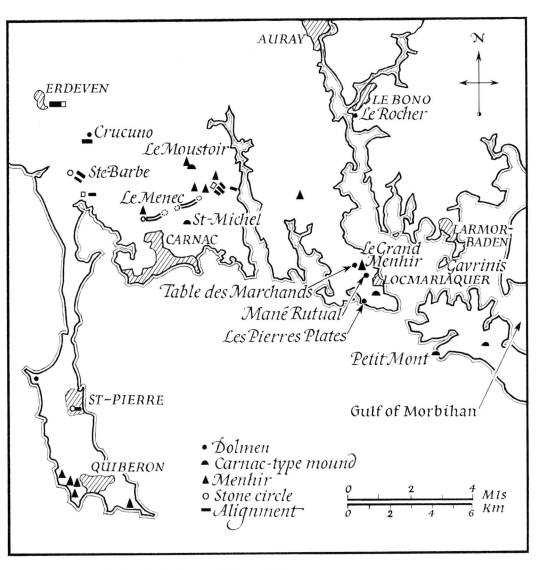

18 Map of some major sites in the vicinity of Carnac, Brittany.

sill lying at the entrance to the chamber bears on one of its faces a chevron like that at Fourknocks, and a number of the designs on uprights resemble those at Newgrange. Clusters of arcs are arranged to make powerful and unique patterns brilliantly related to the forms of the stones and to each other. Some are said to be anthropomorphic; others seem purely abstract. The effect of the ornament is to create an interior space as richly adorned as that of a castle hung

29

with tapestries, or, perhaps, the interior of a seashell coated with mother-of-pearl. It is a space designed for something precious.

There are other strikingly ornamented tumuli in France, but none compare with Gavrinis, where architecture and symbolic ornament complement each other so beautifully. At Les Pierres Plates, however, some of the most evocative single designs are to be seen. An unprepossessing little group of stones next to a picnic site on the sea near Locmariaquer, Pierres Plates contains some delightfully simple designs. At first glance they remind one of faces – peculiarly mournful faces – but on closer inspection they resemble the stylized female figures seen elsewhere in France – statues of a Neolithic goddess.

At L'Ile Longue, Petit Mont, Mané Rutual and Le Rocher, all, like Gavrinis and Pierres Plates, in the Morbihan district of Brittany, there are similar simplified and almost delicate designs. The style, although certainly related to the Irish style (and some say the origin of it), is specific to this area. There is a highly developed sense of proportion along with a certain economy, almost reticence, in the graphics of these Breton tombs. At Pierres Plates in particular, a few lines sensitively placed create a strongly symbolic stone. At Gavrinis a limited repertoire of forms is repeated with subtle variations to brilliant effect, creating a diverse and yet unified series of richly ornamented architectural elements. Newgrange, with its magnificent kerb- and entry-stones and dramatic chamber, Fourknocks with its superb lintels, and perhaps Knowth, are kindred achievements. Just as in archaic societies there was evidently no separation between sacred and secular, so in the work of these Stone Age designers there was no separation betwen symbolic and ornamental art.

In Spain the 'passage-grave' art is found much more rarely on architectural surfaces than on pottery, jewelry and the small flat idols known as plaques. Painted motifs occur more commonly than carved, but in northern Portugal and southern Spain there are carved symbols.

At the Cueva de Menga, Antequera, Spain, there are a few simple, seemingly anthropomorphic, carvings near the entrance to the megalithic 'cave'. At the Dolmen de Soto, near Trigueros, there are a number of suggestive carvings on the orthostats lining the passage. As at Pierres Plates, there is no attempt to relate the carvings to the architectural elements. The circles, arcs, axe-like forms and various enigmatic geometric scribings are placed at varying heights along the passage, as casually as graffiti in a subway. At La Granja de Toniñuelos, near Jerez de los Caballeros, rayed suns much like those at Dowth in Ireland are found on orthostats.

Since many of the Iberian passage graves bear faint traces of painted decoration, it is difficult to assess the role symbolic ornament played as an adjunct to the architecture. The incised designs now remaining may have been only a small part of a scheme of extensive ornamentation such as the designs at Gavrinis, or they may have been added later, randomly, as doodles or afterthoughts or individual invocations.

As they stand today though, the finest Irish and French passage graves appear to have incorporated symbolic ornament into their structures in a planned and sophisticated way. On the orthostats at Gavrinis and the entrance stone at Newgrange the designs are arranged to exploit the form of the stones, covering them entirely. The repetition of motifs creates an ornamental effect without weakening the symbolic power of the designs. The art of the passage graves combines in its masterpieces, such as at Gavrinis and Newgrange, the highly developed artistic and architectural skills of the Neolithic culture. The use of a limited graphic vocabulary effectively placed for design and ritual purposes in sacred spaces marks the beginning of the marriage of art and architecture which continues, despite periods of separation, until this day.

68–72

73–8

NEWGRANGE, CO. MEATH, IRELAND

19 The mound after its recent restoration, photographed at the
midwinter solstice.

20–22 Newgrange: the entrance. The great carved stone blocking
entry to the tomb; the entrance and roof-box; spiral symbols on the
entrance stone.

23 Newgrange: the entrance viewed from the passage in early
winter.

24 Newgrange: the chamber, with the north recess (left)
and east recess (right).

*25, 26 Newgrange: the elaborately carved roofstone in the east
recess.*

27 Newgrange: the grooved upright R21 in the passage.

28 Newgrange: detail of upright L19 in the passage.

29, 30 Newgrange: the northwest side of the mound, showing
kerbstone 52.

30, 31 Newgrange: the northeast side of the mound, showing
kerbstone 67.

KNOWTH, CO. MEATH, IRELAND

32–34 Ornamented kerbstones near the entrance to the eastern tomb.

35 Knowth: detail of a kerbstone.

36 Knowth, satellite tomb next to the main mound: hidden
ornament on the back of an upright slab.

DOWTH, CO. MEATH,
IRELAND
37, 38 The tumulus;
ornament on an upright.

39 Dowth: kerbstone with sun designs.

40 Dowth: detail of an upright inside the tomb, showing a sun design. Cf. 81.

LOUGHCREW, CO. MEATH, IRELAND

41 Cairn I, view along the ruined passage towards the Hill of the
Witch, crowned by another chambered tomb (Cairn T).

42 Loughcrew: entrance to a tomb (Cairn T).

43–45 Loughcrew: carved stones at, respectively, Cairn T, Cairnbane
West and Cairn L.

FOURKNOCKS I, CO. MEATH, IRELAND

46 The chamber, showing the south recess (left) and west recess (centre).

47 Decorated lintel over the south recess.

48 Decorated lintel over the west recess.

49 Fourknocks I: decorated lintel.

50 Fourknocks I: decorated slab.

Overleaf:
51, 52 Fourknocks I: the so-called 'face' carving; and decorated slab
on the west side of the chamber.

BALTINGLASS, CO. WICKLOW, IRELAND

53 Stone basin amid the ruins of a passage grave.

BARCLODIAD Y GAWRES, ANGLESEY, WALES

54 Decorated stones within the passage grave.

BRYN CELLI DDU, ANGLESEY, WALES

55 Standing stone placed at the entrance to the passage grave.
The top half of the megalith bears a worn labyrinth design.

GAVRINIS, BRITTANY, FRANCE

56 Carved uprights lining the passage to the chamber.

Overleaf:
57–59 Gavrinis around the time of the midwinter solstice: view
along the passage towards the chamber; stone sill and distant
entrance from the chamber; sill and chamber as seen from the
passage.

60–61 Gavrinis: the chamber and a detail.

62 Gavrinis: carved upright in the passage.

63 Gavrinis: carved uprights in the chamber.

64 *Gavrinis: carved uprights in the passage.*

65–67 Gavrinis: three views of an upright in the passage.

LES PIERRES PLATES, LOCMARIAQUER, FRANCE

68, 69 Carved symbols inside the passage grave.

70–72 *Les Pierres Plates: decorated stones inside the tomb.*

LA TABLE DES MARCHANDS, LOCMARIAQUER, FRANCE

73 Entrance to the passage grave.

74, 75 Upright at the end of the tomb, decorated with a pattern of
'crooks'. Cf. half-title illustration.

76 Carved stone inside the entrance
to the passage grave.

MANÉ LUD, LOCMARIAQUER, FRANCE

77, 78 Details of carved slabs.

LA CUEVA DE MENGA, ANTEQUERA, SPAIN

79, 80 Entrance to the passage grave; and engraved 'crosses', the
only symbols found inside the tomb.

LA GRANJA DE TONIÑUELOS, BADAJOZ, SPAIN

81 'Rayed suns' carved on an upright slab inside the tomb. Cf. 40.

DOLMEN DE SOTO, NEAR
TRIGUEROS, SPAIN

*82–84 View of the
entrance to the passage
grave; interior; carved
symbols in the tomb.*

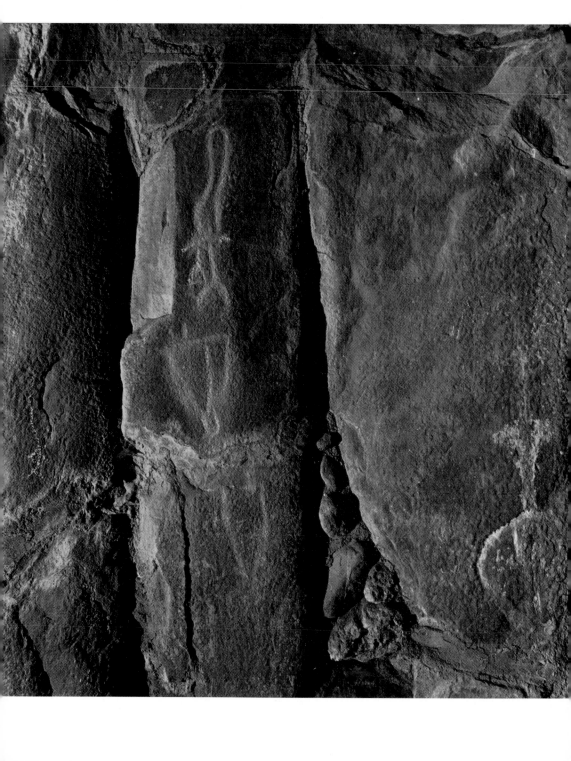

85–89 Dolmen de Soto: symbols carved on slabs inside the tomb.

Cup-and-ring art

Traditionally discussions of Neolithic rock inscriptions have distinguished between the art
associated with passage graves and the variety of
'cup-and-ring' forms which occur on free-
standing boulders or rock surfaces.[1] This is quite
useful for purposes of organization, but the
distinction cannot always be maintained. In the
Canary Islands, for instance, there are 'passage-
grave' symbols on outcrops of rock independent
of any structure (although near caves), and in Irish
passage graves[2] there are cups and rings.

In spite of the exceptions, though, it is possible
to give a general description of cup-and-ring
sites. Such sites, exist, of course, not only in
Europe, but all over the world: India, America,
Africa, Asia. In Europe, especially in Britain, the
carvings are ordinarily found on outcrops not far
from the sea, and there is often a concentration
of carvings in a particular area.

Although simple cup marks – round de-
pressions of varying diameters – are found on
standing stones and other vertical surfaces, more
elaborate variations are most often on horizontal
surfaces. In Spain and Italy, however, complex
designs carved on some vertical stones or stelae
are strikingly similar to the passage-grave
repertoire.

Remembering the exceptions, we can say that
for the most part the symbols on single stones,
stone outcrops and simple rock tombs such as
cists consist of cups and rings and variations.
They range from simple cup marks alone or in
series to elaborate labyrinths and cups surrounded by as many as ten rings, often with a
groove running out from the centre. Map-like
patterns of circles, rounded rectangles and dots
occur in isolation or as part of extensive
concentrations on large outcrops or associated
rock surfaces.

In general these designs do not have the same
formal organization as the work on the great
passage graves. The arrangements show little
concern for the form of the rock itself. Although a
series of concentric circles may be skilfully and
accurately executed, with careful attention to
proportion within the design, the relationship of
one symbol to those adjacent is irregular and
seemingly haphazard. The passage-grave builders, by contrast, appear to have been concerned
in their finest achievements not only with the
execution of a particular symbol, but with the
relationship of that symbol to the others nearby,
to the form of the rock bearing them, and to all
the other carvings as part of a complete design.

The cup-and-ring symbols and their arrangement may differ from the passage-grave repertoire, but the chronology seems to overlap. R. W.
B. Morris,[3] a scholar who has devoted fifteen
years to the study of the cup-and-ring marks in
Scotland, dates the petroglyphs in Argyll to
probably before 1600 BC. Evan Hadingham
characterizes simple cup marks as having been
the oldest and most repeated motif in the
tradition of rock carving in Britain, dating those
on chambered tombs between 4000 and 2000 BC,
those on standing stones and stone circles c.
2500–1200 BC, and those on stones in single
graves c. 2000–1400 BC.

It is, of course, very difficult to date carvings on
isolated stones. Datable organic materials are

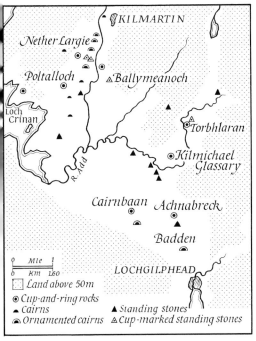

Map with labels:

KILMARTIN
Nether Largie
Poltalloch
Loch Crinan
R. Add
Ballymeanoch
Torbhlaran
Kilmichael Glassary
Cairnbaan
Achnabreck
Badden
LOCHGILPHEAD

0 Mle 1
0 Km 1.60
▢ *Land above 50m*
◉ *Cup-and-ring rocks*
▲ *Cairns*
◩ *Ornamented cairns*
▲ *Standing stones*
△ *Cup-marked standing stones*

90 Map of sites in the mid-Argyll region.

unlikely to survive without protection. Carvings may have been added at different times over the years. Inscribed stones may have been re-utilized, for example as cist covers, in later constructions. Neolithic sites seem to have remained in use for many years, even centuries, undergoing successive structural changes.

Techniques of carving give some indication of general chronology. Both the cups and rings and the passage-grave inscriptions seem to have been pecked out with stone implements. Elizabeth Shee describes the technique she believes was used in Irish passage graves (although no tools have as yet been found in Ireland): the striking of flint or quartz points with a wooden mallet.[4] In Italy quartz tools have, according to Anati,[5] been discovered near the engraved rocks (see below).

There is, as one would expect, less evidence for preliminary planning at cup-and-ring sites than at passage graves. At Newgrange, for example, a lightly picked design was evidently used as a guide for subsequent elaboration. One finds there also the refinement of surfaces by light picking, the use of false relief (picking away the area surrounding a design), and area picking, where the design itself is inscribed in an area already recessed by picking. All these are passage-grave techniques, absent from the cup-and-ring carvings.

A fine example of a concentration of cups and rings is found at Achnabreck, Argyll, Scotland. Here possibly the greatest number of carvings at any one site in the British Isles is clustered on a series of stone outcrops at Achnabreck Farm. A 91 short walk (short, that is, if you have the intuitive powers to interpret the sparse and cryptic signposts) up the hill behind the farmhouse and barns lie three large sheets of rock. Cups and rings, some with comet-like tails, are clustered randomly on these outcrops set in the pine woods with a view of Kilmartin Valley.

Along the length of the valley lies an extensive series of Neolithic remains – standing stones, a large linear cemetery comprising a number of cairns, and numerous carvings on rock outcrops – Nether Largie North, Kilmichael Glassary, Torbhlaran, and Poltalloch besides Achnabreck Farm. It is an area of great beauty – green fields around grey farmhouses, castles (some ruined and others very much alive), churchyards, and narrow roads which lead down to the lakes. Afternoon light, especially in winter when the sun sets early, falls across the fields, throwing into relief the grasses and often a standing stone or stone circle. Brought to life at sunset, such stones are unforgettable.

At Kilmichael Glassary an outcrop has been 96 fenced off across the road from a lovely churchyard. A series of interesting keyhole patterns, quite weathered, have been deeply carved into the schist rock. They are unlike those at Achnabreck – mostly deep cups, none with more than one ring. At Torbhlaran, a few miles up the lane to the north, there is a standing stone with cup marks and two 'whale-backed out-crops' with cups and rings.

93   One of the most extraordinary cup-and-ring sites in Argyll, if not in the whole of Britain, is the one at Ormaig, near Loch Craignish and not far from the Kilmartin Valley. 'Mostly first discovered' by Miss Marian Campbell in 1973,[6] a smooth pinkish rock sheet was stripped of turf to reveal beautifully preserved rosettes and cup patterns. In addition, a small flint graving point and a slate disk somewhat over a centimetre in diameter were discovered on the rock. Were they connected with the carvings? It is possible, even likely, but there is at present no way of knowing for certain.

98   On the hillside surrounding Mr Daniel O'Sullivan's farm house at Derrynablaha, County Kerry, Ireland, inscribed rocks similar to those both at Achnabreck and Torbhlaran are hidden among grasses and ferns. Rock 10 is particularly striking, with cups and concentric rings grooved from the centre like those at Achnabreck.

97   Farther south in Kerry, near Staigue Fort (a fine large stone fort probably of the early Iron Age), lies a rock with unusually simple and careful designs. This outcrop at Staigue Bridge is inscribed with a series of cups, mostly with only one ring, arranged in a cluster. At the far edges of the rock there are isolated cups with one ring, so that the whole does give the appearance of some sort of map, as an early antiquarian, the Reverend Charles Graves, suggested.

Another notable site in County Kerry is near Milltown, not far from the standing stones known as the 'Gates of Glory'. A large boulder lies in a field, with cup marks and designs reminiscent of the keyhole patterns at Kilmichael Glassary.

In England the most important concentrations of cups and rings are found in Yorkshire and Northumberland. The carvings on Ilkley Moor, near the town of Ilkley, Yorkshire, include a few motifs not found elsewhere. A stone described traditionally as the 'swastika stone' bears a design very much like the so-called 'celtic rose' inscribed in Valcamonica, Italy.

In Valcamonica, about 40 miles north of Milan, there are according to Emmanuel Anati about 130,000 rock carvings. In this valley, which lies between Pisogne and Edolo, one can trace eight thousand years of evolving rock art. Diverse historical periods are represented side by side on the same rock.

The carvings which most concern us here belong to the Neolithic (though who could resist the charm of the processions of wheeled carts, the Etruscan figures, the 'scene of the Devil' and the countless other engravings both earlier and later than the Neolithic?), falling within Dr Anati's periods II and III of Camunian rock art: 4000 to perhaps 2800 BC. During this phase the ancient Camunians added cups and rings and other abstract symbols to their earlier repertoire of hunters and animals. One sees a kinship to Neolithic art elsewhere in Europe. For instance, on the stelae now at the Camunian Centre for Prehistoric Studies at Capo di Ponte, there are symbols which could easily be found in an Irish or Breton passage grave. It is clear from the careful research conducted by the Centro Camuno that during the second half of the Neolithic period the emphasis changed from animal and anthropomorphic figures to schematic figures, symbols and abstractions.

Under the leadership of Dr Anati the Centro's studies have revealed much about prehistoric art techniques in Italy. One of the most interesting discoveries is that some of the early schematic carvings could have been executed with stone tools in from three to ten minutes.[7] Thus the carvings could have been done impulsively, even casually. It seems quite possible that in those days one carved at times for fun, which is not to imply that the repertoire of designs was not highly symbolic, even sacred.

Another discovery of interest was that these artists enhanced their carvings with coloured pigments. Anati's investigators have found traces of colouring materials at the base of some of the rocks, and have deduced that 'yellow, red, brown, green, violet, and many other colours as well' were used in ancient times.[8]

Much less attention is being paid to some striking carvings in the Canary Islands. On the island of La Palma an intermittently paved road will, unless the rain falls too heavily, take the traveller to the Fuente de la Zarza at the northern tip. Near the Zarza cave spirals and concentric arcs are carved in profusion on vertical rock faces. It is a lush environment, overgrown with fern and lacy green leaves, soft and spongy underfoot, very different from the more austere landscapes in Ireland and Brittany. Yet the designs have much in common with those at Newgrange and especially Gavrinis, although they are not connected with a megalithic structure. They seem to belong precisely in the middle, between passage-grave art and the cups and rings.

At the Cueva Belmaco, another cave on the same island, there are a number of designs on a large sheet of rock, now broken. This may at one time have been quite differently situated in relation to the cave, but now lies below it in several large fragments. These are carved in a similar, although somewhat more naturalistic, style to those at Fuente de la Zarza.

At the southern tip of La Palma, surrounded by jet-black cinder rock from a recently active volcano, is the Roque de Teneguia. This pale salmon-coloured outcrop high above the sea is carved with a number of spiral designs, many almost too worn to be discerned now.

These carvings, and all the cups and rings found independent of stone structures, seem much more enigmatic than the inscriptions which function, even indirectly, as an adjunct to architecture. They may have been utilized as part of a very specific and/or elaborate ritual or community activity which has left us no clues as to its nature. Lying by the roadside now, or in a field, the stones call up images of tokens or talismans or instruments placed on their surfaces, dances danced round them, songs sung, and the sound of drums.

The simple cup marks on standing stones and the designs on horizontal stones in Great Britain, for example, seem very different from the statue-stelae in Italy and France. Detailed research over many years by Alexander Thom, Emeritus Professor of Engineering in the University of Oxford, has suggested mathematical principles which govern both alignments of standing stones and the cups and rings (see Chapter Five). In addition, the standing stones seem to have served some astronomical purpose.[9] Cup marks may be connected with the ancient use of surveying instruments which could have fitted into the cups or worn them into the stone. Astronomy was no doubt crucial to these people, and may be an important key to the cups and rings.

The designs in the Canary Islands seem closely related to the passage-grave tradition as well as to the cups and rings, perhaps forming a link between the two. It is necessary to evolve still another category, however, when we begin to consider the Stone Age monuments in Malta.

ACHNABRECK, ARGYLL,
SCOTLAND

91, 92 Outcrops of rock carv
with cup-and-ring patterns.

ORMAIG, ARGYLL,
SCOTLAND

93 Rosettes and cups-and-
rings uncovered on a hillsid
overlooking Loch Craignish

94, 95 Ormaig: 'keyhole' patterns on the second rock; and a detail of the main rock (93).

KILMICHAEL GLASSARY, ARGYLL, SCOTLAND

96 Weathered 'keyhole' patterns and cups (some with one ring).

STAIGUE BRIDGE, CO. KERRY, IRELAND

97 A series of cup-marks, mostly within single rings, clustered on a rocky outcrop near an Iron Age fort.

DERRYNABLAHA, CO. KERRY,
IRELAND

*98 Daniel O'Sullivan and one of his
dogs at Derrynablaha Farm.*

*99, 100 Close-up and distant views of
rock 10.*

BAILDON MOOR, YORKSHIRE, ENGLAND

101, 102 Cup-marked stone originally found lying flat, but now set into concrete near the north wall of the Dobrudden Farm Caravan Park.

ILKLEY MOOR, YORKSHIRE, ENGLAND

103 The Swastika Stone (replica, bottom right).

104 The Panorama Stone, found originally on the moor but now preserved opposite St Margaret's Church, Ilkley.

105 The Hanging Stones seen from below.

106–108 The Hanging Stones, Ilkley Moor: details and general view.

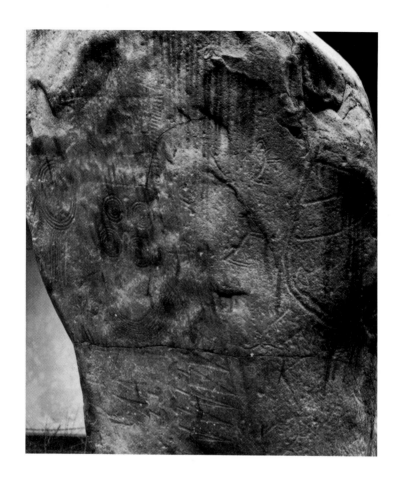

VALCAMONICA, LOMBARDY, ITALY

109 Carved boulder from Borno, now in the Museum of
Archaeology, Milan. The first 'monumental composition' to be
discovered in Valcamonica.

110 The 'Map of Bedolina', a carved rock face thought to show
buildings, fields, paths and streams.

111–113 Valcamonica: carved stelae now in
the Camunian Centre for Prehistoric Studies, Capo di
Ponte (respectively Bagnolo I, Bagnolo II and
Ossimo I).

114–116 Valcamonica: decorated rock surfaces at Luine.

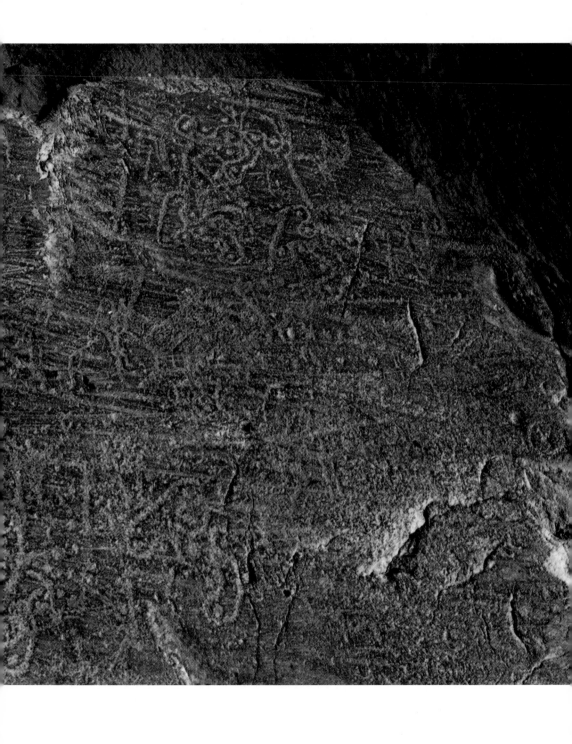

FUENTE DE LA ZARZA, LA PALMA, CANARY ISLANDS

117–119 Cliff face carved with concentric arcs and circles. Cf. 63–67.

120, 121 Fuente de la Zarza: carved rock faces.

ROQUE DE TENEGUIA, LA PALMA, CANARY ISLANDS

*122, 123 Distant view of the rock at the southern tip of La Palma;
worn spiral design on an outcrop.*

CUEVA BELMACO, LA PALMA, CANARY ISLANDS

124 Design carved on a rock.

Maltese ornament

Fifty miles south of Sicily, in the Mediterranean Sea, lie what the eminent prehistorian Gordon Childe[1] called 'the barren little islands', Malta and Gozo. It is true, there are no forests here, only stones. But what stones! The islands' vast deposits of limestone were used even before 3000 BC to create some of the earliest monumental architecture.

During the Neolithic period[2] a series of megalithic (and one 'megalithic-style') structures were built which are architecturally unique. They remain, even ruined as many now are, among the most evocative of monuments. They were constructed of giant stones, which enclosed curved rather than rectangular spaces. The basic plan consists of pairs of oval chambers budding from a central passage, or a simple trefoil arrangement.

The ornamental carving (and occasionally painting) in the interiors and courtyards of these structures is of a delicacy and sophistication unparalleled in megalithic art. Although the builders used a fairly hard coralline limestone for the outer walls, blocks for the interiors were cut from soft globigerina. Since this type of limestone is easy to work, especially when it is first cut, early carvers were able to use their stone tools to create flowing and yet precise designs.

The main motifs of this art are curvilinear (especially the circle and spiral and occasional other geometric abstractions), and naturalistic – fish, bulls and other animals. The curvilinear motifs dominate, and are perhaps the most interesting because of the way in which they enhance the architecture of the 'temples'.

Although 'temples' is a term which comes easily to mind when we see the megalithic edifices in Malta, we should not imagine that their use was exactly equivalent to our use of churches or cathedrals today. The monumental buildings no doubt served for rituals of every kind: birth, death, the movements of the sun and moon, harvests and sacrifices.

The plan of the complex of buildings at Mnajdra, for example, gives us a sense of these rituals. Here, on the southwestern edge of Malta, is one of the simplest and most beautiful ruins. There are three temples, built at different times and at varying levels to one side of a nearly round forecourt. A terrace separates this court on the other side from a steep slope down into the Mediterranean. The spaciousness of the forecourt seems perfectly suited to large gatherings – perhaps dances, processions and communal celebrations of the rhythms of life.

At Mnajdra the only ornament (except for a crudely carved representation of a megalithic building on one orthostat in the upper 'temple') is the regular drilling of holes into many of the stones. Some of these pitted stones are arranged to form niches or 'altars'. Although the drilling may have been for purposes other than ornament, and certainly could not be regarded as a symbol, it is nonetheless extremely effective as a decoration.

Not far from Mnajdra is one of the most impressive of all the Maltese buildings, Ħaġar Qim. Here three smaller curved structures are surrounded by a single wall. The orthostats in this wall are enormous, forming an awesome façade through which one enters into spaces arranged on a much more intimate scale.

Little megalithic art has been recovered from Haġar Qim, although some may have been lost during early destruction conceived as 'excavation'. One of the few finds is a 'blocking slab' carved with 'oculus' or eye-like spirals. Such slabs, bearing two spirals which remind us of eyes, are used at other sites as well to form knee-high barriers to interior chambers.

Another find is a miniature pillar, unique among the Maltese remains. It is stylistically peculiar, carved on each of its four faces with a naturalistic plant form unlike any other motif from this period. This plant 'grows' out of a decoratively drilled tub similar to another discovered at Tarxien, a fine site near Valletta. The whole of the pillar is drilled as well, and carved to simulate four trilithons.*

Simulation of the trilithon technique of building has been carried to its most sophisticated level in the 'megalithic-style' structure beneath an urban section of Malta, Hal Saflieni. Here workmen excavating for a building project in 1902 discovered an incredibly beautiful and well-preserved series of underground chambers. Pressed by the owners of the project to conceal the discovery lest it interfere with their building plans, workmen inflicted considerable damage to the upper levels – another blow struck against the Maltese archaeological heritage.

Called the 'Hypogeum' (meaning 'under the earth'), the structure consists of a series of chambers on several levels, carved from the bedrock. Here, still quite legible, are the only paintings from the Neolithic period, decorative curvilinear tendrils and disks on the walls and ceilings. The designs are similar to many of the carved motifs remaining on exposed weathered

* 'Trilithon' is used to describe the particular 'doorway' formed by three great stones in megalithic architecture: a slab at each side surmounted by another slab across the top of the opening.

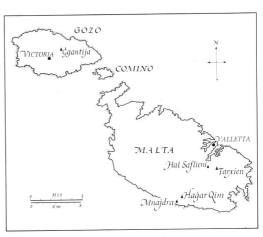

125 Map of Malta and Gozo, showing sites mentioned in the text.

surfaces of megalithic buildings elsewhere in Malta.

Although the motifs in the Hypogeum resemble those carved elsewhere, the effect is different. On the ceiling of a room called 'the oracle chamber', a series of spirals is painted expressively in red ochre, giving the effect of a plant form or 'tree of life'. In other chambers hexagons and semi-spirals, sometimes combined with disks, cover the walls and ceilings with a graceful curling pattern. Lacking the finesse and sophisticated precision of the limestone carvings elsewhere, the paintings are nonetheless most appealing in their naïvety and casual grace.

Besides painted decorations, the Hypogeum offers a great deal to the visitor. There is, for example, one chamber – called the 'Holy of Holies' – where an entire 'megalithic-style' façade is carved into the rock: lintel, uprights and corbelled ceiling. The work is masterful – finely tooled, beautifully proportioned. There is an ochre wash on the walls, and on the floor a V-shaped depression, with stone plugs, which could have received a liquid offering.

Excavation of the adjoining chambers brought to light human bones, ornaments and offerings.

132

134

Dr Themistocles Zammit, the principal excavator, calculated that between six and seven thousand individuals had been buried here.[3] Further, in the National Museum, Valletta, one can see in addition to the major decorated stones from other sites a wonderful 'Sleeping Lady' discovered in the main chamber of the Hypogeum. Although other figurines were discovered here, including another, less appealing, sleeping lady, this one, lying on her simple couch, is the most delightful. Tiny (12.2 cm long) yet monumental, she reclines peacefully as though she were a goddess receiving a dream. There has been some guesswork about the possibility of a 'dream cult' connected with the structures. Perhaps, like a vestal virgin, or better, a queen bee, this goddess in human form fed on titbits and delicacies, lived in the temple, and dreamed rich dreams for the priests to interpret.

Although no Hypogeum has been found as yet on the neighbouring island of Gozo, old legends have it that there was such a cave beneath the major megalithic monument there, the Ġgantija. Excavation has uncovered no subterranean passage, but there are very large worn spirals remaining on blocks of stone. Other blocks are drilled and/or carved, some with remains of plaster. At the National Museum there is a block with spirals carved in relief, the background painted red.

The finest and most extensive carvings in Malta are preserved at the large group of buildings known as Tarxien, very near the Hypogeum of Hal Saflieni. Here four 'temples' built in successive periods remain in various stages of ruin and preservation, and there is evidence that at one time the remains spread even more widely.

Entrance to the series of temples is made through the forecourt of the South Temple. It is elegantly paved and decorated, dominated by the skirt and dainty feet (a replica of a National Museum original) which are all that remain of a goddess who must once have had the same monumental form as the 'Sleeping Lady' of the Hypogeum – though this figure is measured in metres not centimetres. Near the massive goddess are a series of blocks carved with spirals and a lovely altar also ornamented with running spirals. In the altar is a niche, formed by removing a plug from the centre of the block and hollowing out a space. Excavators found in this space a flint knife-blade and a goat horn. Above, another niche in the same altar yielded a number of goat bones, suggesting that sacrifices were made at this spot.

In the adjacent Central Temple there is a central passageway, with three pairs of apses or side chambers (some with carvings) branching off from it. The most striking element here is the oculus sill-stone which blocks the doorway into the inner chambers. Inside are two extraordinary slabs serving as screens to opposite apses. The originals are in the custodian's house, and represent one of the finest achievements of Maltese megalithic art. They are boldly and precisely carved, strongly ornamental, simple and yet sophisticated. On each a series of four spirals is carved in relief around a central disk, yet the two screens are not identical, for the spirals curl inward on one, and outward on the other. Why does the entry to the western apse bear spirals turning in towards each other, and the eastern apse spirals turning away from the centre?

Whatever the answer, it is at Tarxien that one can see most clearly the sense of design which makes Maltese ornament unique. Perhaps because the soft limestone was so workable, the execution of symbolic motifs has a verve and preciseness not seen elsewhere in Neolithic art. It is in addition a highly evolved system of ornament, where relationships between repeated motifs are carefully worked out, and care is given both to these interrelationships and to the whole form of the block on which they are found.

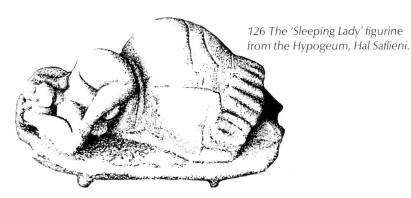

126 The 'Sleeping Lady' figurine from the Hypogeum, Hal Saflieni.

Thus the style encompasses not only a specific facility of placement and carving, but the ability to create a powerful unified architectural whole. The forms and techniques used to create the great stone structures are refined and adapted to express the same sensibility in interior ornament. It is only in the Hypogeum that we see a marked stylistic division between structural stonework and decoration, in this case painted.

In Malta one can study a skilled and beautifully decorative ornamental art, which is not to say that its symbolic content was any less powerful or profound than that more laboriously carved elsewhere. Nor are the basic symbols so different. As in passage-grave art, the curvilinear element is most common: spirals, concentric arcs and circles, and disks or cups are found everywhere. Although there are many naturalistic plant and animal forms, in Malta the axe-form so common elsewhere is missing.

In summary there is no doubt that the Maltese combination of architecture and symbolic ornament is a great achievement in the history of art and architecture. Although the chronology seems to be in a constant state of flux, these structures are roughly contemporary with, if not somewhat earlier, than those in Ireland and Great Britain, and later than some carved structures in Brittany – that is, they belong by and large to the early third millennium BC.

The striking aspect of this Neolithic period is that in such widely separated areas as Malta, France, Great Britain, Italy and the Iberian peninsula as well as in Scandinavia and other parts of the world, an abstract symbolism arose and to a good measure replaced the naturalistic art of the Palaeolithic caves. Thus at the time that prehistoric folk began to settle, to farm, and finally to build, they began to evolve a symbolic graphic 'language'. This is not an alphabetic language, but a language of symbols which may have had similar although not identical meanings from culture to culture. The implications of this will be discussed in Chapter Six.

Although in Malta the only use of concealed decoration seems to be the drilled holes on the reverse of some blocks, and may be due to their re-use, elsewhere symbolic carving occurs on concealed surfaces. On the backs of inaccessible kerb-stones and orthostats in Irish passage graves, and inside cist covers in Germany and Great Britain, there are symbols only the ghosts could see. This may all be the result of decorating stones before incorporating them into structures, or re-using important carved pieces. It is, however, one more similarity between widely separated cultures.

After surveying the major megalithic sites in Europe, as well as the cup-and-ring concentrations, what then? We need to ask why the symbols were carved, what significance they had for prehistoric people. But first we should look at what has been written of these things, and at what the archaeologists have to tell us.

MNAJDRA, MALTA

127 Two slabs and massive lintel forming a 'trilithon' doorway.

128 Detail of 127, showing the drilled ornament to the left
of the doorway.

HAĠAR QIM, MALTA

129, 130 'Pillar' or 'altar' and detail , showing a naturalistic plant motif unique in Maltese megalithic art.

131 Monumental entrance, with slabs of weathered globigerina limestone.

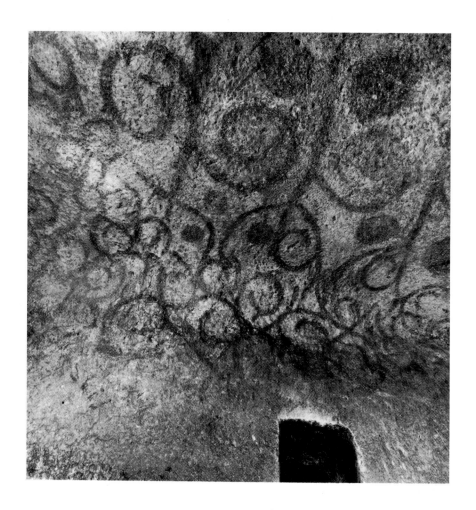

HYPOGEUM, HAL SAFLIENI,
MALTA

132 Ceiling of the 'oracle
chamber', with a tendril design
painted in red ochre.

133 Hexagonal designs on the
wall of a chamber adjoining the
'oracle chamber'.

134 One of the main halls in the
underground 'temple', carved out
of limestone to resemble a
megalithic façade.

TARXIEN, MALTA

135 View southeast over the second chamber of the Central
Temple. Note the carved screen (replica of 136) in the middle
distance.

136 Carved screen from the Central Temple, now in the custodian's
house.

137 Tarxien: western apse of the South Temple after a rainstorm.

*138 Tarxien: eastern apse of the South Temple, dominated by the
skirt and legs of a massive goddess, whose upper half was destroyed
by farmers before the site was excavated. Cf. 139.*

139 Tarxien: another view of the mother goddess in the South
Temple. Cf. 138.

140 Tarxien: spirals in the western apse of the South Temple.

141 Tarxien: reconstructed altar in the eastern apse of the South
Temple.

142–144 Blocking slabs from (top to bottom) Bugibba, Tarxien and Ħaġar Qim.

145–147 Tarxien: carved limestone blocks.

Antiquarians, archaeologists and astro-mystics

Before the nineteenth century there were no archaeologists, only 'antiquarians'. These were usually men of broad interests and considerable learning, some keepers of museums and others physicians or lawyers or just plain aristocrats. They travelled widely, poking into ruins and seeking out interesting 'antiquities'.

It was a Welsh antiquarian, Edward Lhwyd, who first visited and described the tumulus at Newgrange in 1699, soon after its discovery by workmen carrying off stones for the use of 'the Gentleman of the Village (one Mr Charles Campbel)'. He thought the site 'some place of sacrifice or burial of the ancient Irish' and described the stones as 'rudely Carved, [having] such barbarous Sculpture (viz. Spiral like a Snake, but without distinction of Head and Tail)'[1] that it seemed to indicate that it was a 'Barbarous Monument', and thus pre-Roman.

One of the first official records of the 'barbarous' inscriptions was an entry in Camden's *Britannia* (Gough Edition, 1789) where a plate opposite page 603 shows a stone with cups and rings, described as a 'Druidical altar, discovered lying on the ground near the Rev. Mr. Hart's at Lynsfort or Inis Oen, 1773. The greatest length is 28 feet, in breadth 25. It is full of rock basons ... [and one corner] is a block on which the human victims were slain.'[2] The next edition, published in 1806, has a lengthy description of the 'celebrated mount or pyramid formed of pebble or coggle stones' at Newgrange, including this reference to the inscriptions:

On the flat stone which forms the north side of the left-hand niche Governor Pownall [Quaker ex-Governor of Massachusetts] discovered what he took for traces of

letters ... As they are reducible to no known alphabet, but come nearest to the Phoenician, he supposed the stone brought from some old monument of that people on the sea-shore here. Colonel Vallancey [another antiquarian] comparing it with the druidical Ogham reads it Aongtus, a common name of Irish kings and here of the arch-druid; but the Governor cannot deduce such a reading from the Ogham. On some of the stones which form the sides and backs of the kistvaens he found lines cut in a spiral form: in the front edge of one of the stones forming the top of the kistvaens some lines forming a kind of trellis-work in small lozenges, such as are not unfrequently found in Danish monuments and crosses. The Governor inclines to think this barrow sepulchral, the cave at the end the cemetery, and the three kistvaens or tabernacles repositories of three several persons of different ranks, whose ashes were collected and laid in the rock basons. Dr. Molyneux [another antiquarian] says *two entire skeletons* not burnt were found on the floor in the cave when it was first opened: Colonel Vallancey only *one*, and that it lay on the large stone at the center, and no other bones but black ashes in the three niches. He deems it a tomb built by a Druid in his life-time, who offered sacrifices in it, and thence he calls it Antrum Mithrae; but the Governor maintains that it is a Danish monument formed successively as the persons interred in it died, and the Inscriptions brought from another place.[3]

William Wakeman, in the first edition of his *Handbook of Irish Antiquities* (1848) describes and illustrates a 'great variety of carving, supposed by some to be symbolical'. He comments on the inscription illustrated in *Britannia*:

An engraving upon a stone forming the northern external angle of the western recess is supposed to be an inscription; but, even could any satisfactory reading of it be given, its authenticity is doubtful, as it has been supposed to have been forged by one of the many dishonest Irish antiquaries of the last century.[4]

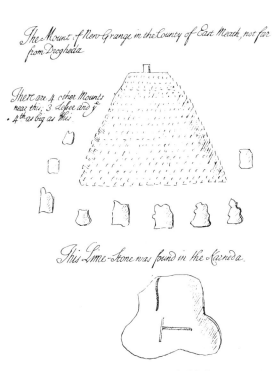

The Mount of New Grange in the County of East Meath, not far from Drogheda

There are 4 other Mounts near this; 3 lesser and ye 4th as big as this

This Lime-Stone was found in the Karneda.

148 A drawing of Newgrange, probably by Edward Lhwyd, who visited the site in 1699.

He remarks on the similarity of a leaf design on the same stone to one found on a tomb in Brittany, and notes that some of the inscriptions must, because of their inaccessible location, have been carved before the stones were placed.

Around 1851 the Reverend Charles Graves in Ireland and the Reverend William Greenwell in Northumberland, England, were among the first investigators of cups and rings. Since in both countries the discoveries were near Iron Age forts, it was natural to guess that the rings were primitive maps, locating nearby forts. Greenwell also suggested that the cups might denote burial sites.

Evan Hadingham recounts a number of interpretations which followed the 'map' theories – astronomical observations or beliefs, star charts, signs used by early prospectors looking for metal ores.[5] George Tate, in 1865, discarded plans of camps or doodling as possibilities, arguing that the carvings were religiously symbolic.[6] More recently Ronald Morris has catalogued some of the explanations offered for Scottish cups and rings, including 'adder lairs, knife-sharpening holes, moulds for metals, sex-rites, masonic marks, grinding mills, anvil-stones, lamps, early writings, and the druids.'[7]

With the advent of what we now know as archaeology in the mid-nineteenth century, less attention was given to imaginative interpretations of megalithic symbols. Archaeologists, perhaps because their training and interests tended to be more specialized than those of the antiquarians, collected data: types and locations of designs, tools and techniques, grave goods and artifacts, chronology.

Abbé Henri Breuil, eminent early archaeologist and authority on cave art still somewhat in the tradition of the antiquarians, presented his views on megalithic art to the Prehistoric Society of East Anglia in 1934.[8] He organized the repertoire of passage-grave symbols and cups and rings into stylistic and chronological categories. The symbols originated in Iberia, he felt, and were nearly all representations of the human form. These anthropomorphic designs spread to Brittany, Scandinavia, Britain and Ireland, meanwhile undergoing stylistic changes relating to location and chronology. Professor R. A. S. Macalister, then a leading archaeologist in Ireland, collaborated with Breuil on much of the latter's work there, seeing in the carvings battlefields, severed heads, goddesses, and

For the lozenges, ... they represent the head of the bull-roarer, the sacred instrument almost universal in primitive mysteries. Concentric circles with a radial line closely resemble the labyrinthine patterns which find their highest expression on the coins of Crete; and so these may perhaps suggest a place for ceremonial dances, and thus the sacred dance itself.[9]

149 'Routing Linn Inscribed Rock', from George Tate's Ancient British Sculptured Rocks of Northumberland and the Eastern Borders (1865).

As Hadingham points out,[10] some of the rock markings fancifully interpreted as battlefields were later found to have been entirely natural results of erosion and weathering. However, there were enough clear resemblances between the designs found in Spain and northern Portugal and those in Britain for Eoin MacWhite in 1946 to distinguish between two styles: 'passage grave' (originating in southern Spain) and 'Galician' (brought from northwestern Iberia and perhaps originating in the East Mediterranean).[11] Although the work of Breuil and MacWhite and others represented a valuable and painstaking study of the evidence, their conclusions, which

supported a diffusionist theory of prehistory – that cultural advances spread from one or two sources and could be traced back to those using archaeological clues – were thrown into disarray by scientific advances in dating. I have mentioned the 'radiocarbon revolution' described by Colin Renfrew, which occurred when advances in correcting radiocarbon dating revealed the sources to be more recent than their so-called derivatives. Passage graves in Brittany now antedate their 'precursors' in Iberia.

There are, then, stylistic similarities between Iberian and French or Irish megalithic art, and between other widely separated Neolithic cul-

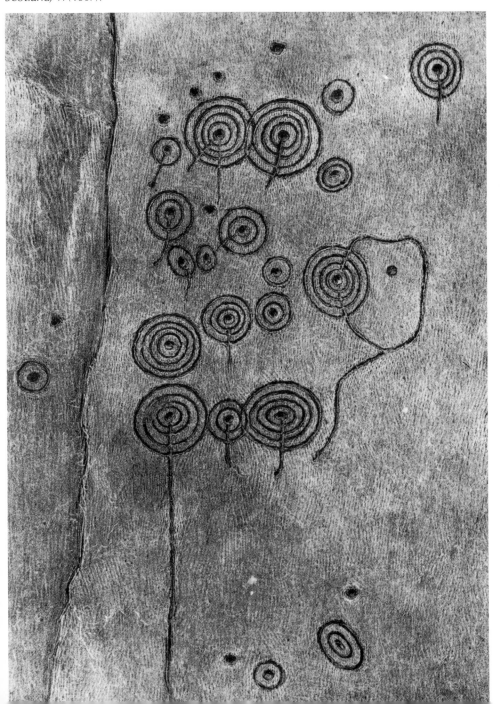

150 Cups and rings on a rock at Cairnbaan, Argyll, from an article by
J.Y. Simpson in the Proceedings of the Society of Antiquaries of
Scotland, VI (1867).

tures, which cannot be accounted for by simple patterns of diffusion. Whether this implies that the patterns of diffusion must be seen as more complex, perhaps deriving from two or more original 'centres', must be balanced against the possibility that the Neolithic mentality, and indeed the universal human mentality, tends to manifest itself in a similar fashion everywhere in the world.

Although megalithic art is certainly the most striking manifestation of the Neolithic mentality, archaeologists in general have tended to treat it as an interesting but peripheral aspect of the cultures which built the great tombs. Glyn Daniel, however, one of the most distinguished British prehistorians, sees that

apart from Upper Palaeolithic and La Tène art, the art of prehistoric man has received very cursory treatment . . . The study of prehistoric art is . . . one of the few ways in which the prehistorian can get towards the non-material values of the people he studies, and perhaps catch a glimpse, however fleeting, of the intellectual adventure of prehistoric man.[12]

Outside Britain early archaeologists such as Oscar Montelius concentrated upon establishing 'avenues of influence' (such as that of Cretan designs upon Irish passage grave art), later demolished by the correction of radiocarbon dates. Joseph Dechelette, whose *Manuel* is a basic document in French archaeology, argued that Iberia was the source of a cult of female divinities, whose eyes and eyebrows were represented by spirals such as those at Gavrinis and Newgrange.[13]

In Germany Herbert Kuhn studied European rock art beginning with the Ice Age. He distinguished early naturalistic from later stylized forms, using Spanish symbols as an example of the latter.

The symbols are so simplified, so conventionalized, so nearly reduced to symbols that they look, for all the world, like some sort of script or writing.[14]

Although European Neolithic art did not develop

into writing, Kuhn felt that the use of such symbols constituted a 'spiritual advance', signalling the turning of human attention to such elements of existence as fertility, health, chance and the preservation of life. He offers

a key to the understanding of the rock pictures during the second and first millennia BC [now dated earlier]. The figures are not those of ordinary men. They are those of ghosts. They are not ordinary beasts . . . they are ghostly beasts. All these rock-pictures . . . are witnesses to a general belief in spirits permeating all the realms of existence . . . and are therefore marked by an estrangement from the real world around us.

If we can say that the first great epoch of prehistoric art is characterized by hunting- and sympathetic-magic, so the art from the third millennium onwards might be called that of the epoch of animism and myth. The men of this period developed concepts of mysterious and superior Powers, of a nature that is living and animated down to its smallest components, and also beliefs in survival after death and in the influence of the spirits of the dead.[15]

Megalithic rock art in Germany is comparatively rare, but a slab from a grave at Göhlitzsch, Sachsen-Anhalt, bears a textile-like design.[16] T. G. E. Powell and others have taken this to represent wall-hangings or decorations, and Powell traces such a tradition back to funerary practices in ancient Russia.[17]

In Italy Emmanuel Anati has, as we have seen, made a careful analysis of the thousands of inscriptions in Valcamonica and elsewhere. From the Stone to Bronze Ages he sees a change in mythology and religion, beginning with the solar cults and symbols of tools, moving to anthropomorphic divinities and 'megalithic-type' symbols (snake patterns, meanders, zigzags, concentric disks and so on), to pantheistic and cosmological religion.

In the last phase, between the Stone and Bronze Ages, the compositions inscribed were

the result of a school of art with precise laws of composition, aesthetics, and symbolism. The monuments were conceived and planned before being made, and show a technical mastery undoubtedly of artists who knew their trade well, and who in modern terminology would be defined as 'professional artists'. Obviously these people had a highly developed aesthetic sense which changed from period to period. However, both the conclusions drawn from the analysis of the Camunian rock carvings and the numerous pertinent ethnological parallels, seem to indicate that 'art for art' never existed in prehistoric Valcamonica, that the carvings were aimed at magical-religious functions and that their execution was considered as part of the activities vital to the group in ensuring successful economic and social outcomes, and good relationships with the occult forces of 'beyond'.[18]

In general, then, throughout Europe, antiquarians and, later, archaeologists, began by cataloguing and analysing the repertoire of megalithic inscriptions on structures and free-standing stones in order to trace their origins in far-off lands such as Iberia and the East Mediterranean. When the new methods of dating were developed, much of this work seemed to have been wasted. Yet what strikes the layman who simply wants to find out more about megalithic art is that the descriptions and observations remain valid, however shattered the conclusions. And what emerges as exciting is the fact, as Evan Hadingham points out, that

The appearance of these designs [cups and rings] not merely in Europe but all over the world, among ancient traditions as widespread as those of Brazil, India and Australia, indicates the fundamental nature of the impulse to create these simple abstract forms.[19]

Outside conventional archaeology, however, there are those who are willing to risk extraordinary and, to many, incredible interpretations. These range from the painstakingly researched ideas of Alexander Thom, mentioned briefly in Chapter Three, to the far-fetched speculations of Erich von Däniken, who offers 'pictorial evidence for the impossible'.

Thom, together with other members of his family, has spent many years studying the geometry and astronomy of British and French stone circles and alignments. It is his work which

has been primarily responsible for the development of another concept contradicting the traditional view of prehistory – the idea that 'primitive' prehistoric human beings possessed systems of measurement and observation which allowed them to construct geometric figures of a sophistication perhaps not yet fully understood by modern mathematicians.

The existence of a standard unit of measurement in Britain, which he calls the 'megalithic yard' about 83 cm, or 2.7 ft), seems to have been demonstrated by Thom (although I hasten to add that there is not general agreement on this point in archaeological circles). In studying Scottish cup-and-ring marks, Thom suggests that they were set out with a unit of 1/40 megalithic yard (2.07 cm, or 0.816 in.), which he calls a 'megalithic inch'. He states that

the underlying principles and terms of reference controlling the standing stone non-circular rings are identical with those in the cup and ring non-circular* designs. It is certain that whereas the former were set out with measuring rods and ropes the latter needed accurate dividers and an accurate scale of megalithic inches.[20]

Analysing a number of the Scottish non-circular rings, he finds a geometry based on specific 'esoteric' megalithic terms of reference. He suggests the possibility that the Pythagorean Theorem may have been known to these people.

The implications here are interesting. If the standing stones and rings are designed as a result of astronomical criteria, does the fact that the cups and rings follow the same rules imply that they have to do with astronomy? Thom suggests they do in a 1965 article. In his foreword to R. W. B. Morris's book on the Scottish designs, however, he asks, referring to the cup-and-ring marks, 'Do they contain a message? Are they the beginning of a form of writing?'[21]

* By 'non-circular' Thom means the apparently circular 'rings' in megalithic geometry: standing stones, concentric rings and so on, which are actually flattened ellipses.

Thom's work makes a strong case for a complex and sophisticated megalithic geometry developed independently from other 'cradles of civilization'. Less scholarly minds have advanced Egypt as the source of megalithic mathematics and symbolism. Grafton Elliot Smith, Professor of Anatomy in Cairo at the turn of the century, propounded with little semblance of scientific method the hyperdiffusionist view that all civilization derived from Egypt.[22] In this he was followed by his disciple, W. J. Perry,[23] and more recently by John Ivimy, in *The Sphinx and the Megaliths*, with specific reference to Britain. Ivimy's 'pyramidiocies' (as one archaeologist has called them) include the notion that Stonehenge was built by visiting Egyptian priests who needed a foreign observatory.

Less exotic is the suggestion that megalithic spirals and concentric arcs such as those at Gavrinis represent the lines of human fingers or palms. This idea was put forward by Eugene Stockis in 1921[24] and later in *Fingerprint and Identity Magazine* by Bridges (1937).

More recently there has been a spate of writers well versed in melodrama, who are not afraid of leaping to astonishing conclusions, unaided by scholarly references. Although their flair for the arresting conclusion seems more a matter of faith than of science, not the least of their achievements has been to arouse the traditional archaeologists to poetic heights of creative indignation. 'A tarradiddle of rubbish and nonsense', 'brittle insubstantial crackpots', they rage, and not without reason.

Robert Charroux is one such author given to provocative speculations. In *One Thousand Years of Man's Unknown History*[25] he states his thesis that our 'Superior Ancestors' were much more highly advanced in science than we, having developed nuclear power, space travel and a secret alphabet hundreds of thousands of years ago. Various conspiracies throughout history have kept these facts from us.

Erich von Däniken, perhaps the best-known writer of this 'archaeological science fiction', poses questions like this (referring to rock inscriptions): 'Were they the earliest communication to fellow tribesmen of contacts with extra-terrestrial beings?'[26] Francis Hitching, in *Earth Magic*,[27] is more cautious, although the style of his book is somewhat similar. He relies on the ideas of earlier exponents of ley lines, alignments traced through various ancient monuments and landmarks such as standing stones and sacred structures. Such lines have been said to represent invisible forces or fields, and were first suggested by Alfred Watkins in the 1920s. Later writers such as Guy Underwood and John Michell have explored what Michell calls 'the old system of spiritual engineering' and 'the mysterious currents upon which depended the entire civilisation of the ancient world'.[28]

Hitching's book suggests that prehistoric man may have had powers of divination like those which water dowsers possess in modern times. Or rather, Hitching says that dowsers such as Scott Elliot (a President of the British Society of Dowsers 'for some years') and Bill Lewis, a dowser from South Wales, make this suggestion. Lewis, according to Hitching, proposed the possibility that the 'stone power' – that force which dowsers sense – emerged from the ground beneath a standing stone in the form of a spiral.

Reading a book like *Earth Magic* is less than satisfying because the author seems to have collected a mass of data which includes an enormous amount of hearsay and rubbish as well as reliable evidence, and no distinction is made between the two. Thus the experience of a 'well-known psychic' of whom we've never heard, who fell into a fit of dizziness before a certain stone, is presented side by side with the views of Alexander Thom, who has taken great care to pursue a scholarly and scientific line of research.

What one is left with is a sense of a gap between the careful accumulation of archaeological data and details and a factless flight into realms of mystic possibility. We long for some sense of the importance of the symbols from Neolithic sites. For, as Evan Hadingham writes, 'The most essential and exciting point is the growing evidence that the lozenges, spirals, cups, and circles of Britain may represent the first major west European art tradition since the Ice Age.'[29]

Not only the evidence that megalithic symbols may represent a major tradition in art, but the sense that they represent concrete evidence of the state of the Neolithic mind, provides a strong motivation for continuing to look, even outside the boundaries of archaeology and astro-mysticism, for answers to the many unresolved questions.

CHAPTER SIX

Possibilities

Megalithic architecture and the symbols inscribed upon stone in Neolithic times are the
most direct physical evidence remaining to us of
the ancient symbol-makers. And if our study of
those symbols so far has disclosed little or
nothing of the tenor of the mind, or the language,
or the culture of Neolithic people (and I think that
the three are inseparable), perhaps what there is
to be learned about the nature of language and
of the mind itself will reveal, at last, something of
the meaning of the symbols.

Bearing in mind Sir Peter Medawar's aristo-
cratic warning that a 'large population of people,
often with well-developed literary and scholarly
tastes, who have been educated far beyond their
capacity to undertake analytical thought', are
likely to fall prey to unscrupulous or careless
'experts',[1] still I find it difficult to resist further
exploration. Contemporary developments in
linguistics and semiotics, neuro-physiology and
even physics, as well as studies in comparative
religion and anthropology, can be explored for
answers to questions about the symbols.

First let us consider whether the symbols
constitute a form of 'writing'. For many years it
was customary to think of 'cave' inscriptions –
especially Palaeolithic art, but also the geometric
symbols associated with megaliths – as 'pictorial
writing'. Later a distinction was made between
this *pictographic* art – when an image represents
only the object it portrays and nothing more –
and that which is called an *ideogram*.

The ideogram symbolizes something more or
something different from the concrete object it
depicts. A rayed circle as a pictogram could

represent 'sun', while as an ideogram it might
represent 'heat' or 'day'. An essential characteristic of pictorial writing, both pictograms and
ideograms, is that there is no connection
between the image and its spoken equivalent for
the object or idea signified. Phonetic values are
ignored.

Since we have no idea of the languages spoken
in the Stone Ages, can we agree with the linguists
that the signs have no phonetic associations? I
think so, if only for the obvious reason that their
arrangement is so limited. It is difficult to
conceive of a language with as few different signs
occurring in a given geographic area. Of course it
is possible that the inscriptions represent only a
tiny percentage of the total vocabulary, that
which was reserved for sacred purposes. There
may have been other signs painted, scratched
into dirt or carved on to wooden tablets. Even so,
the arrangement of the symbols, random or
clearly decorative and/or repeated as patterns,
implies that the carvings are ideograms, representing an evolution from the simpler pictograms
of Palaeolithic cultures.

The next phase in the evolution of pictorial
writing is the refinement of fixed conventional
signs to correspond to a quite precise and un-
equivocal meaning.[2] It is here, I think, that the
symbols fall into place in the evolution of writing
– as refined, specific, evolved ideograms which
could symbolize both concrete objects (such as
the axe or the sun) and abstract ideas (such as the
spiral may have represented).

Although 'in some ancient cultures the
stylized pictures of the Neolithic led on into

writing ... The decisive factor that was present in ancient Mesopotamia, Egypt and China was lacking in neolithic Europe', according to Herbert Kuhn.[3] This missing factor, he believes, was the existence of a priest class which could interpret the signs. As I have mentioned earlier (Chapter Two), archaeologists such as MacKie and Herity believe that there was indeed such an élite class of priests and astronomers, who passed on complex knowledge such as that required to arrange and erect the megalithic observatories. However, for whatever reason, Neolithic symbols do not seem to have led on directly to a system of phonetic writing, the way early Sumerian pictograms, for instance, evolved into cuneiform.

That this ancient European graphic art remained symbolic and did not evolve into writing cannot be considered a handicap to the spiritual and cultural development which took place during the Neolithic. As the famous French anthropologist Claude Lévi-Strauss puts it, '... writing, while it conferred vast benefits on humanity, did in fact deprive it of something fundamental'.[4] Lévi-Strauss cites the positive effects in 'non-civilized' societies of personal relationships, concrete relations between individuals. He points out that direct links with the past through oral traditions have been replaced by books, that direct connections between individuals and rulers or governments have been replaced by the media.

Most importantly, what has been lost to humanity with the invention of writing is the archaic capacity for explaining the world around us by establishing analogies between nature and human life. Intuitive 'mythic' logic and observation of nature made the world comprehensible in a different way from the rational abstract modes of thinking we now use. If we accept the structuralist characterization of what Lévi-Strauss calls the 'savage mind' and believe, as he does, that although the *mode* of operation of archaic minds was different, the nature of both the archaic and 'civilized' minds remains the same, what can this tell us about the Stone Age symbols?

In *Structuralism and Semiotics*[5] Terence Hawkes discusses the applications of structuralist thinking to semiotics, the science of signs. What emerges of importance to the study of Stone Age symbols is the inter-relationship of all aspects of a culture, including the structure of its language. This structure is not specific, limited, and varying from one language to another, but is universal to human beings throughout the ages. There are, then, universal principles governing human language which 'derive from mental character-istics of the species'.[6]

Cultural anthropologists such as Lévi-Strauss extend this idea, asking

whether the different aspects of social life (including even art and religion) cannot only be studied by the methods and with the help of concepts employed in linguistics, but also whether they do not constitute phenomena whose inmost nature is the same as that of language ...[7]

The study of Stone Age symbols thus becomes the study of the total culture of these 'primitive' human beings. Nor were such 'primitives' barbaric and ignorant as we once supposed; as the Italian jurist and philosopher Giambattista Vico pointed out as long ago as 1725, they were instinctively 'poetic' in responding to their environment. An inherent 'poetic wisdom' ordered their responses to the world and cast these responses into a 'metaphysics' of myth, symbol and metaphor.

Thus 'childish', 'primitive' beliefs and customs represented not ignorance, but sophisticated and serious ways of encoding and coping with reality. The first science to be learned, according to Vico, is that of myths or fables, and all myths represent the 'actual generalized experience of ancient people'.[8] The form these myths impose on the world springs from the human mind itself, and reflects it.

It follows, then, that in the end, the language, the myths and eventually the societies and institutions created by human beings can be said to participate in creating those human beings themselves. Thus a 'human physics' evolves, in which poetic truth is metaphysical truth and objective reality ceases to signify.

This is the structuralist view, perhaps over-simplified. The Stone Age symbols, if one accepts this view, surely represent the Stone Age beliefs. Whatever the specific functions of megalithic structures, whatever the particular meaning of the decorated stone in the field, they are manifestations of the culture and thus the metaphysics of Neolithic people – their met-aphors, symbols and myths.

As Vico pointed out, 'with our civilized natures we [moderns] cannot at all imagine and can understand only by great toil the poetic nature of these first men.'[9] One key, it seems to me, to understanding this 'poetic nature' is found when we turn our attention to the symbols themselves, and how they differ from alphabet writing.

First, symbols are *esoteric*, whereas words are *exoteric*. That is, symbols imply without specify-ing exactly. They refer to an innate or intuitive knowledge without formulating (and thus limit-ing) a concept. Words, on the other hand, refer to formulated concepts, and are static. Because a word begins with an abstraction which refers back to the object, rather than signifying through evocation, magical analogues and so on, it is considered by R. A. Schwaller de Lubicz, an expert on Egyptian symbolism, to be more of a 'dead end'. It does not lead to poetic wisdom or 'elicit an abstract vital response'. The symbol, by its powers of evocation, can serve as a synthe-sizer. It can exist outside time, representing an abstract reality which can be comprehended intuitively, but never objectively expressed.

Schwaller de Lubicz explores these attributes using Egyptian hieroglyphics. What pertains to the study of Neolithic symbolism is the idea that

archaic symbols refer to magical analogues in order to express that 'poetic wisdom' outside contemporary logic. Thus one does not seek dictionary definitions of such symbols, trying to anchor them to words like 'rebirth' or 'sacred'. It is necessary, rather, to consult comparative religions and ancient sacred texts based on beliefs which existed before writing, in addition to simply looking at the symbols themselves.

According to Mircea Eliade, an authority on comparative religions, the main difference be-tween modern and archaic human beings lies in the strong connection the latter feel with the 'Cosmos and the cosmic rhythms', while the former feel (or claim to feel) a connection only with history. (Of course there is a 'sacred history' connected with the Cosmos, and this is pre-served and passed on through myths.) Another distinction Eliade likes to emphasize is that between the religious experience of archaic man and the non-religious 'desacralized' experience of modern man. Noting that 'the completely profane world ... is a recent discovery in the history of the human spirit', Eliade observes

that desacralization pervades the entire experience of the nonreligious man of modern societies and that, in consequence, he finds it increasingly difficult to rediscover the existential dimensions of religious man in the archaic societies.[11]

Examining what scholars like Eliade and Joseph Campbell[12] consider to be some of the basic myths of archaic human beings, we must remember that we will not find exact equivalents for the terms that have arisen in philosophy and religious traditions. 'But if the word is lacking, the *thing* is present: only it is "said" – that is, revealed in a coherent fashion – through symbols and myths.'[13]

What, then, are some of the basic beliefs of what is called 'the savage mind'? Eliade separates archaic belief, based on 'various groups of facts, drawn here and there from different cultures',[14] into several different categories.

First, the 'celestial archetype'. For archaic people, reality imitates a celestial prototype. In ancient traditions, both Eastern and Western, temples and sacred spaces, cities and the whole world shaped by men and women have a prototype which exists on a higher cosmic level. But wild, uncultivated, uninhabited regions do not have such prototypes: they reflect the primordial chaos, the formless state of Pre-Creation.

Thus the settlement of a new territory is a symbolic repetition of the act of Creation, and rites are performed which repeat this 'cosmicizing'. The participation by communities and urban cultures in an archetypal model is what validates them. The rites of Creation transform chaos into cosmos; ritual makes inhabited territory 'real'.

'Real' in this sense means 'sacred'. For the archaic mentality, reality consist of 'force, effectiveness, and duration'.[15] Only the sacred creates and causes things to endure – hence the primitive concern for acts of consecration.

Together with their belief in archetypes, archaic human beings embraced a series of beliefs in the symbolism of the 'Centre'. The 'Sacred Mountain', where heaven, earth, and hell come together, is located at the centre of the world. Every sacred city, temple or palace is a Sacred Mountain, and thus a Centre. Cities and sacred places are located at the summit of the Sacred Mountain, the highest point of the earth and at the same time the navel of the earth. Of course this is an oversimplification of the ancient concept of the temple as a reflection of the world, reproducing the essence of the universe, an idea still surviving in some religions today.

Absolute reality exists at the Centre; it is the territory of the sacred. Symbols of absolute reality (and here Eliade cites trees of life and the fountain of youth as examples of such symbols) must be located at a Centre. The road to the Centre is difficult, hazardous, labyrinthine.

The interior chambers of passage graves such as Newgrange and Knowth in Ireland could be said to be situated at a Centre, and the spirals at the entrances could represent, at least in part, the road to the Centre, from death to life, from the profane to the sacred, from illusion to reality. Arriving at such a Centre is a consecration, initiation into the real, the enduring, the effective.

Since every creation represents the original Creation, a sacred space such as a megalithic structure would have to be founded at the centre of the world, consecrated as such, and carefully located according to the beliefs prevailing at the time. Thus placement of the megaliths could have been determined by astronomy (see the description of Alexander Thom's work in Chapter Five and of the winter solstice at Newgrange, Chapter Two), geomancy (see the discussion of ley lines, Chapter Five), and/or other magical factors.

It is interesting to speculate on the possibility that spirals, parallel lines, circles and arcs may symbolize a 'force' which has not only a mythic reality (as in the Polynesian concept of mana, a life force) but is closely connected with forces now acknowledged in modern physics – sub-atomic electromagnetic particles which transcend Newtonian laws and the precepts of nineteenth-century scientific thought.

Can the proven effectiveness of dowsers and their divining rods have some connection with these forces, as Guy Underwood and others have suggested? Did such forces play some role in determining the location of ritual centres? Eliade refers to the 'geomantic theories that govern the foundation of towns', and certainly geomancy was a powerful science in ancient times. As yet, connecting the Neolithic spiral with electromagnetic forces is pure speculation. Perhaps modern physics, as it advances along what seems to be a path away from traditional scientific logic towards a paradoxical 'poetic' description of a world of particles which are neither mass nor force yet both, will explain these spirals to us one day.

A sacred site, whether selected by geo-mancers, priests, astronomers or all of these, must be consecrated to secure its sacredness, and thus its reality. 'Through the paradox of rite, every consecrated space coincides with the centre of the world, just as the time of any ritual coincides with the mythical time of the "begin-ning".'[16] Concrete, profane time is transformed into mythical time, profane space into transcen-dent space. Any ritual, then, is performed not only in a sacred space, but in a sacred time, the original time of the divine Creation.

Each ritual – circumcision, marriage, sex and so on – reflects a divine archetype. Every significant act – food-gathering, hunting, cooking, games and so on – connects with the sacred. It is in that sense a ritual, created for the first time by a divinity: 'an ancestor, a totemic animal, a god or a hero', in the timeless mythical period, 'those days'. Even war was a ritual function, repeating an episode of the divine cosmic model. All the important acts were first revealed and enacted by gods or heroes, and archaic human beings only repeat these archetypal gestures over and over forever.

A key set of concepts regarding time is grouped by Eliade into a category he calls 'The Regeneration of Time'. Divisions of time were determined by rituals governing the food supply, guaranteeing the continuation of the whole community and its life.

The solar year is of Egyptian origin. 'The majority of other historical cultures – and Egypt itself down to a certain period – had a year, at once lunar and solar, of 360 days. (that is, 12 months of 30 days each), to which five intercalary days were added.'[17] The beginning and length of the year may have varied considerably, but in every culture the end of one period and the beginning of the next was significant, was based on biocosmic rhythms, and formed part of a system of rituals – periodic purifications and the periodic renewal of life. Most importantly, this periodic regeneration of time implied a new Creation, and thus abolished 'history'.

Regeneration involves the casting out of sins, diseases and devils, and is an attempt to recreate at least for that moment the mythical primordial time. There is a new birth for the community and for the individual, and the moment of passage from chaos to cosmos is repeated once again.

Fires are kindled each year in many cultures at the time of the winter solstice, and the orien-tation of the Newgrange passage grave to this solstice has already been mentioned. In Malta the summer solstice seems to have been considered in siting the megalithic structures, and the large forecourts certainly seem designed for ritual activities. It is not difficult to imagine the ritual opening and/or entering of a megalithic space each year at one or more of the solstices. Perhaps the ashes of the year's dead were interred at the time, returning the soul to a sacred state.

Time, for Neolithic folk, must have been con-tinually renewed, even within the 'year'. The moon was important to this renewal, connected in primitive myths with death and resurrection, birth and fertility, and so on. The phases of the moon, which have been shown to have in-fluenced megalithic construction, were import-ant in evolving cyclical ideas. Lunar myths establish shorter rhythms (weeks, months) and serve as symbols for longer durations such as solstices, years or astronomic cycles, and for the possibility of renewal even in the face of famine or other catastrophe. The 'lunar perspective' implies that individual death and even the periodic death of humanity are as necessary as the three days of darkness which precede the rebirth of the moon.

This archaic sense that time was regenerated in the same way as the sun and moon seem to regenerate themselves has been replaced by our belief in history, and in the finiteness of time. We feel at every moment the sense that time is slipping by, that death is final and inevitable. Much of our lives is spent in avoiding this idea, in finding diversion. The megalith builders, by contrast, erected their most enduring monuments for burials or to house the ashes of their dead relatives or chiefs. Because their actions repeated divine prototypes, they saw them as significant, and 'real'.

Among archaic people, there seems to have been a nostalgia for a lost paradise – a distant time when there was a bountiful supply of food to be gathered with little effort, when there was neither death nor suffering. In 'those days' (what the Australian aborigines call so beautifully 'the Dreamtime'), heaven and earth were in closer communication, mortals mounted to heaven and gods descended to earth with ease. 'As the result of a ritual fault, communications between heaven and earth were interrupted and the gods withdrew to the highest heavens. Since then, men must work for their food and are no longer immortal.'[18]

Working for food, that is, cultivation of plants, seems clearly associated with veneration of Mother Earth, a vital concept in Neolithic culture. She is a very old divinity in both Eastern and Western religions, known since Palaeolithic times. The Earth Mother embodies all forms of fertility – human, agricultural, animal – and her mythology is susceptible to unlimited enrichment and variation. She may represent an androgynous creator, undifferentiated, neither feminine nor masculine, a 'creative wholeness'. Or she may be the universal womb to which Neolithic dead were returned, buried in the embryo position.

The 'goddess' of Maltese megalithic 'temples' is a particularly evocative example of a Neolithic Earth Mother. Her huge likeness at Tarxien, mutilated though it is, remains a powerful feminine presence in the forecourt of the temple. Yet her skirt is not so different from those of the more masculine 'priest' figurines discovered there, and she does not seem particularly sexual. There are many depictions of the goddess sleeping. Could her fertility have been a richness of imagination, her function that of dreamer of symbolic or oracular dreams?

There are countless examples of the Neolithic goddess engraved on plaques and stones, and there have been attempts to see her in even the most abstract symbols. She is clearly an important element in Neolithic beliefs, but there is no evidence, according to Eliade, that she was the only divinity. He points out that besides worship of the Earth Mother a whole galaxy of complementary or seemingly incompatible beliefs could exist.

From Palaeolithic times caverns had a religious meaning connected with the Earth Mother. In megalithic architecture, the cave was constructed and no doubt ritually transformed into a labyrinth, which was both a 'theatre of initiation and a place where the dead were buried'. In turn the labyrinth represented the Earth Mother, and entering the labyrinth or cave was a mystical reunion with the Mother. Marriages too were celebrated in labyrinths, as were symbolic sacrifices.

The spiral or labyrinth is one of the most fascinating of the Neolithic repertoire of symbols. It encloses space, implying a path or flow between the lines. It has already been suggested that this may symbolize the flow of some form of energy. Perhaps it is the path of the spirit, or as Theodore Schwenk suggests, the 'flow of the forces of speech'.[19]

In *The Origin of Consciousness in the Breakdown of the Bicameral Mind*, Julian Jaynes makes the interesting suggestion (without, I think, convincing proof) that ancient men and women did not possess the powers of introspection, reflection and judgment that we do today. Their responses were guided, he feels, not only by instinct but by hallucinated voices they heard as the voices of the gods. If this were true, the symbols could represent such messages in graphic form, an idea not unlike Schwenk's above and perhaps not inconsistent with the idea of 'spirit-' or 'force-paths'.

An aspect of archaic thinking which persists today has to do with sacred objects. It is clear that a stone or a tree may be sacred. Eliade reminds us that the stone or tree in itself is not worshipped: the sacred is manifesting itself in a stone. The paradox here that is common to all religious phenomena, from a standing stone to the symbol of Christ, is that by making itself manifest the sacred is limiting itself and giving up its quality of absoluteness. Accepting that all manifestations of the sacred are equivalent, with much the same meaning, 'we then realize that there is no essential discontinuity in the religious life of mankind'.[20]

These 'archaic realities' are described by Mircea Eliade extensively in his works on comparative religion. I have given only a brief sketch here, but it seems to me that they must be considered in a study of the Neolithic symbols.

Does this mean that, armed with the ancient mythologies, one could sit down and compile a dictionary of Stone Age symbols? I think not, for many reasons. For one thing, the Late Stone Age or Neolithic took place in many different locations and at many different times, and the communities, cultures, and thus the symbols, must have varied. Stone Age tribes exist in faraway places even today, although they are a scarce and endangered breed. Their beliefs, while they may provide a clue to the prehistoric, will of course not be exactly the same.

Secondly, symbols are not equivalent to words, and they may convey meanings words cannot express. Words in one language are themselves not exact equivalents of words in another.

Finally, although we can come much closer to understanding the frame of the archaic mind through the work of anthropologists such as Lévi-Strauss and historians such as Eliade, there is no proof that a given symbol has a specific significance. Our guesses only become more sophisticated, and, perhaps, more satisfying.

After making a pilgrimage – either through studying photographs or travelling or both – and reading relevant theories in linguistics and anthropology and the history of religion as well as the archaeological data, what then? What do we know?

For me, the striking revelation has been the seriousness of purpose of archaic men and women, manifested again and again in their symbols and structures. In changing from hunting and gathering to farming, the people of the Neolithic formed more or less permanent communities and settlements. Their art, in becoming more abstract, seems to reflect a turning of the mind towards contemplation, towards the world of the spirit, towards the meaning of life and death.

By carving into stone, by moving great boulders into place, they took part in the creation of their environment, and thus their lives, and at the same time they created a world for their dead. The symbols were the language of that world, the 'real' or sacred world in which they lived during the significant moments of their lives and into which the dead were reborn.

As symbols, the Stone Age designs contain meanings which could not be precisely translated into our language, even if we had a Neolithic symbols Rosetta Stone. It is for this reason that photographs are invaluable in attempting to transmit some sense of the symbols to the reader. Black-and-white photographs have a certain capacity to strip away the effects of time, to act as a kind of telegram from the ancients, allowing us to ignore the sound of traffic on a nearby highway. The photograph tends towards direct experience, although it is never truly 'objective'.

What is possible, and ultimately most valuable, is that we can simply look at these symbols without formulating an explanation. They are messages from fellow human beings, messages which have survived long after time has burned away the organic paraphernalia of everyday life which must have surrounded them. As Schwaller de Lubicz suggested, 'to cultivate oneself to be simple and see simply' is to move closer to an intuitive understanding of these symbols. As we come to understand them, we can perhaps begin to discover something of the nature of our archaic forebears, and what still remains of the sacred in ourselves.

Notes

CHAPTER ONE

1 Colin Renfrew, *Before Civilization* (Harmondsworth 1976), p. 161.
2 See A. Thom, *Megalithic Sites in Britain* (Oxford 1967), G. Hawkins and J. White, *Stonehenge Decoded* (London 1966) and J. E. Wood, *Sun, Moon and Standing Stones* (Oxford 1978) for information about megalithic mathematics and astronomy.

CHAPTER TWO

1 Both M. Herity (whose excellent book, *Irish Passage Graves* (Dublin 1974), is valuable for many aspects of the subject) and E. MacWhite ('A new view on the Irish Bronze Age rock scribings' in the *Journal of the Royal Society of Antiquaries of Ireland*, vol. 76 (1946), pp. 59–80) describe these forms extensively.
2 Evan Hadingham, *Ancient Carvings in Britain: a Mystery* (London 1974), p. 28.
3 See G. Coffey, *New Grange and Other Incised Tumuli in Ireland*, first published in 1912, now reissued by Dolphin Press (1977), p. 30. This is a classic work on Newgrange and worth reading.
4 Claire O'Kelly, *Illustrated Guide to Newgrange*, rev. edn (Blackrock, Cork 1978) pp. 111–12.
5 For details, see Herity 1974.
6 See Herity 1974, p. 123.
7 Knowth, Dowth and Newgrange, like most ancient sites around the world, have at some time (if not repeatedly) been plundered. The Vikings apparently left notations at Knowth and Dowth around AD 861, and it is assumed that other more ancient people disturbed the deposits as well.
8 Herity 1974, p. 126.
9 M. Herity and G. Eogan, *Ireland in Prehistory* (London 1977), p. 53; Euan MacKie, *Science and Society in Prehistoric Britain* (London 1977).
10 For megalithic construction methods, see S. Piggott, *Royal Institute of British Architects Journal*, vol. 63 (1956), pp. 175–80, and R. Atkinson, 'Neolithic Engineering', *Archaeologia* (1961), pp. 292–9.

CHAPTER THREE

1 See MacWhite 1946 (ch. 2 n. 1 above). He presents the view that the cups and rings are a distinct ornamental repertoire, originating in the 'Galician'

inscriptions occurring in the north of Spain and Portugal.
2 Hadingham 1974, p. 72.
3 Morris has published a catalogue of the carvings in Argyll as a preliminary to a more extensive work treating the petroglyphs in southern Scotland as a whole. This catalogue, *The Prehistoric Rock Art of Argyll* (Poole 1977), is invaluable to the cup-and-ring seeker in Argyll.
4 E. Shee, 'Techniques of Irish Passage Grave Art', *Jutland Archaeological Society*, Denmark, 1969.
5 E. Anati, *Evolution and Style in Camunian Rock Art* (Edizioni del Centro, Capo di Ponte, Italy 1976), p. 56.
6 Morris 1977, p. 112.
7 Anati 1976, p. 65.
8 Anati 1976, pl. 34.

CHAPTER FOUR

1 Childe was a pioneering archaeologist whose *The Dawn of European Civilization* was first published in 1925, and is still in print.
2 Michael Ridley, in his *The Megalithic Art of the Maltese Islands* (Poole 1971) has revised earlier dating sequences and suggests using 'Neolithic' to describe the years between 4200 and 2000 BC (page 18).
3 See D. Trump, *Malta: An Archaeological Guide* (London 1972), p. 64. Dr Trump's guide is an excellent companion, indispensable for the visitor who wishes to explore Maltese archaeology.

CHAPTER FIVE

1 Lhwyd is quoted at length in Coffey 1912 (1977), pp. 20–21.
2 William Camden, *Britannia*, Gough Edition (London 1789), p. 645.
3 Quoted in Herity 1974, p. 13.
4 W. Wakeman, *Archaeologia Hibernica: A Handbook of Irish Antiquities, Pagan and Christian, especially of such as are easy of access from the Irish Metropolis* (London 1848), pp. 26–7. A second edition, much larger, was published in 1891, and republished by Kennicott Press, New York 1970.
5 Hadingham 1974, pp. 44–51.
6 G. Tate, *The Ancient British Sculptured Rocks of Northumberland* (Alnwick 1865).
7 R. W. B. Morris, 'The Cup and Ring Marks and Similar Early Sculptures of Scotland', Part 2,

Transactions of the Ancient Monuments Society, 16 (1969), pp. 37–67.

8 Henri Breuil, Presidential Address, *Proceedings of the Prehistoric Society of East Anglia*, VIII (1934), pp. 289–322.

9 R. A. S. Macalister, *Ireland in Pre-Celtic Times* (London 1921), pp. 232–3.

10 Hadingham 1974, pp. 77–8.

11 MacWhite 1946 (ch. 2 n. 1 above).

12 Glyn Daniel, *One Hundred and Fifty Years of Archaeology* (London 1975), p. 321.

13 Joseph Dechelette, *Manuel d'archéologie préhistorique, celtique et gallo-romaine*, vol. 1 (Paris 1908).

14 H. Kuhn, *The Rock Pictures of Europe* (London 1966), pp. 99–100.

15 Kuhn 1966, p. 105.

16 See Waldtraut Schrickel, *Westeuropaische Elemente im Neolithikum und in der Frühen Bronzezeit Mitteldeutschlands* (Leipzig 1957).

17 T. G. E. Powell, *Prehistoric Art* (London 1966), p. 123.

18 Anati 1976.

19 Hadingham 1974, p. 79.

20 Alexander Thom, 'The Metrology and Geometry of Cup and Ring Marks', *Systematics*, vol. 6 (1968), p. 178.

21 Morris 1977, p. 5. Thom suggests that the cupmarks were often used in association with standing stones for fixing calendar dates in *Vistas in Astronomy*, VII (1965), p. 55.

22 Sir Grafton Elliot Smith, *The Migrations of Early Culture* (1915) and *Human History* (1929).

23 W. J. Perry, *The Children of the Sun* (1923).

24 Eugene Stockis, 'Les Empreintes Palmaires' and Bridges, 'Personal Identification through the Ages', quoted in Harold Cummins and Charles Midlo, *Fingerprints, Palms and Soles* (New York 1961).

25 New York 1970 (first published in French, 1963).

26 E. von Däniken, *In Search of Ancient Gods* (London 1976), p. 181.

27 London 1976, New York 1978.

28 J. Michell, *The View over Atlantis* (London 1973), p. 161.

29 Hadingham 1974, p. 74.

CHAPTER SIX

1 Quoted by Stuart Piggott in *Antiquity*, vol. 52 (1978), p. 62.

2 For a discussion of the evolution of writing see David Diringer, *The Alphabet* (London and New York 1949) and Ernst Doblhofer, *Voices in Stone* (London 1973), to whom I am indebted for these distinctions.

3 Kuhn 1966, p. 102.

4 Claude Lévi-Strauss, *Structural Anthropology* (London 1968), p. 365.

5 Terence Hawkes, *Structuralism and Semiotics* (Berkeley 1977).

6 Noam Chomsky, *Reflections on Language* (New York 1975), p. 4.

7 Lévi-Strauss, *Structural Anthropology*, p. 353.

8 See Hawkes 1977, pp. 12–13, for an explanation of Vico's and Lévi-Strauss's positions.

9 Giambattista Vico, *The New Science*, quoted in Hawkes 1977, p. 12.

10 For these distinctions and a discussion of the symbolic I am indebted to R. A. Schwaller de Lubicz, *Symbol and the Symbolic* (Autumn Press, Brookline 1978; first published 1949).

11 Mircea Eliade, *The Sacred and the Profane* (New York 1959), p. 13.

12 Joseph Campbell, *The Masks of God: Primitive Mythology* (Harmondsworth 1976).

13 Mircea Eliade, *The Myth of the Eternal Return* (Princeton 1954), p. 3.

14 Eliade 1954, p. 3.

15 Eliade 1954, p. 11.

16 Eliade 1954, p. 20.

17 Eliade 1954, p. 51. Eliade quotes Rock, 'Das Jahr von 360 Tagen und seine Gliederung', *Wiener Beiträge zur Kulturgeschichte und Linguistik*, I (1930), pp. 253–88.

18 Eliade 1954, p. 91.

19 Theodore Schwenk, *Sensitive Chaos* (New York 1976), p. 133.

20 Mircea Eliade, *Myths, Dreams, and Mysteries* (New York 1975), p. 125.

21 Julian Jaynes, *The Origin of Consciousness in the Breakdown of the Bicameral Mind* (Boston 1976).

ACKNOWLEDGMENTS

Thanks to my friends and travelling companions Douglas Muir, Naomi Weissman, Ina Evans and Norma and Gordon Ashby for many forms of support, to Professor Waldtraut Schrickel, Ed Rossbach, Paul Bishop, William Garnett, Michael Smith and Arthur Kitching for hospitality and/or inspiration, and to the staff of Thames and Hudson for their help and encouragement throughout.

Select bibliography

ANATI, EMMANUEL. *Evolution and Style in Camunian Rock Art.* Capo di Ponte, Italy 1976. One of many good books written on rock art by Anati.

BREUIL, HENRI. Presidential Address, *Proceedings of the Prehistoric Society of East Anglia,* VIII (1934).

CAMPBELL, JOSEPH. *The Masks of God: Primitive Mythology.* Harmondsworth 1976.

COFFEY, GEORGE. *New Grange and Other Incised Tumuli in Ireland.* Poole 1977.

DANIEL, GLYN. *The Megalith Builders of Western Europe.* London 1958. Now out of date, but probably still the best introduction to the subject of megaliths.

ELIADE, MIRCEA. *Myth of the Eternal Return.* Princeton 1954.

—— *The Sacred and the Profane.* New York 1959.

—— *Myths, Dreams, and Mysteries.* New York 1975. Eliade's books are invaluable to anyone interested in the history of religion.

HADINGHAM, EVAN. *Ancient Carvings in Britain: A Mystery.* London 1974. An excellent and readable survey of Neolithic and some Bronze Age inscriptions in Britain – the most valuable of all the books I have listed for anyone interested in the subject.

—— *Circles and Standing Stones.* London 1975.

HARBISON, PETER. *Guide to the National Monuments of Ireland.* Dublin 1975. Any visitor to Ireland should have this.

HAWKES, TERENCE. *Structuralism and Semiotics.* Berkeley 1977. Concise and easily understood by a non-linguist.

HERITY, MICHAEL. *Irish Passage Graves.* Dublin 1974. A well-illustrated book.

HERITY, MICHAEL, and EOGAN, GEORGE, *Ireland in Prehistory.* London 1977.

O'KELLY, CLAIRE. *Illustrated Guide to Newgrange.* Blackrock, Cork 1978. Claire O'Kelly and her husband, Professor M. J. O'Kelly, are the foremost authorities on Newgrange.

KUHN, HERBERT. *The Rock Art of Europe.* London 1966.

LÉVI-STRAUSS, CLAUDE. *The Savage Mind.* London and Chicago 1966. An important book for anyone who wishes to understand the prehistoric mind.

—— *Structural Anthropology.* London 1968.

MICHELL, JOHN. *The View Over Atlantis.* London 1973. Michell's point of view is regarded scornfully by traditional archaeologists, but his book is worth reading even by sceptics for its learned and elegant presentation of his views.

MORRIS, R. W. B. *The Prehistoric Rock Art of Argyll.* Poole 1977. Clear directions and excellent organization make this extensive survey most valuable to the visitor to Argyll – use it as a field-guide.

RENFREW, COLIN. *Before Civilization.* London and New York 1973 (Harmondsworth 1976).

RIDLEY, MICHAEL. *The Megalithic Art of the Maltese Islands.* Poole 1971. A complete survey.

TCHOU (editor). *Guide de la Bretagne mystérieuse.* Paris: Les Guides Noirs, 1966. A guide to menhirs, megalithic structures and assorted wonders in Brittany.

TRUMP, DAVID. *Malta: An Archaeological Guide.* London 1972. An excellent guidebook to the most interesting sights on Malta and Gozo.

Index

Numerals in *italics* indicate illustration numbers

abstract symbolism *see* symbolism
Achnabreck Farm 89, 90, *91–2*
alignments, stone 11, 143, *9, 11, 12*
altar, at Mnajdra *5*; pillar from Hagar Qim *129, 130*; at Tarxien 120, *141*
Anati, Emmanuel 89, 90–1, 142–3
Antequera, Cueva de Menga 30, *79, 80*
anthropomorphism 23, 29, 139, 142, *51*
antiquarians 90, 138–9, 143
archaeologists 11, 26, 27, 139–43
archaic beliefs 147, 149, 150, 152
archetypes 149
architecture, at Dolmen de Soto 30; at Fourknocks 28; at Gavrinis 30; at Newgrange 23
arcs 23, 24, 27–9, 91, 121, 144, 149; *see also illustrations under* Bagnolo I, Borno, Fuente de la Zarza, Gavrinis, Knowth, Loughcrew, Newgrange
Argyll (now Strathclyde), Scotland 88; Achnabreck Farm 89, *91–2*; Cairn at Nether Largie Farm *4*, map 90; Cairnbaan *150*; Kilmichael Glassary 89–90, 96; Ormaig 90, *93–6*; Torbhlaran 90
art, abstract 90, 142–3, 152; both symbolic and ornamental 30, 121; in Germany 142; in Italy 90, 142–3; in Malta 118, 120; La Tène 142; passage-grave 23, 28, 139, 140, 142; similar to language 147; *see also* cup-and-ring art, cups-and-rings
astro-mystics 144–5

astronomy 11, 91, 139, 143, 149
Avebury 11, *11*
axe forms 30, 121, *109, 111, 142*

Bagnolo I *111*; II *112*
Baildon Moor *101, 102*
Baltinglass 26, *53*
Barclodiad y Gawres 28, *54*
basin stones 25, 26, 28, *24, 53*
Bedolina, Map of *110*
Borno boulder *109*
Breuil, Abbé 23, 139
Britain 23, 89, 121, 139, 140, 144, 145; abstract symbolism in 121; British designs as major art tradition 145; cups-and-rings in 88; dating of stone tombs 12; idea of Egyptian origin 144; passage-grave style in 28; *see also* England
Britannia, Gough Edition, 138
Brittany, France 11, 138–40; Carnac 11, *9* (Le Menec); chamber tombs 12; Gavrinis 23, 28–30, *56–9, 60–7*; L'Ile Longue 30; Mané Lud *77–8*; Mané Rutual 30, *76*; Pierres Plates 30, *70–2*; Roche-aux-Fées *7*; Table des Marchands *74, 75*
Bronze Age 142
Brugh na Boinne 23; *see also* Newgrange
Bryn Celli Ddu 28, *55*
Bugibba, blocking stone *142*
burial mounds *see* tumuli

cairn at Nether Largie Farm *4*
Cairnbaan, Argyll *150*
cairns *see under* tumuli
Camden's *Britannia, see Britannia*
Campbel, Charles 138
Campbell, Joseph 148
Campbell, Marian 90
Camunian Centre for Prehistoric Studies, Valcamonica 90, *111–13*
Canary Islands, Spain 88, 91; *see also* Cueva Belmaco, Fuente de la Zarza, Roque de Teneguia

Carnac 11, *9*
carving, styles 27, 28, 91; techniques 24, 89, 118
cave art 11, 23, 139
ceilings, Newgrange 6, *25, 26*; oracle chamber, Malta *132*
'celtic rose' 90, *114*
cemetery, prehistoric 27–8, 89
Centre, symbolism of 149
Charroux, Robert 144
chevron *see* zigzag
Childe, Gordon 118
chronology, comparative 121, 140; in Malta 121; in Italy 90; of cups-and-rings 88–9; radiocarbon dating 11–12
circles, discs, rings 139; concentric 140, 142; in Canary Islands 91; in cup-and-ring art 88, 90; in Italy 90, 142; in Malta 118, 119, 120, 121, 146, 149; in passage-grave art 23; in Spain 30; 'non-circular' rings 143 *see also illustrations under* cups-and-rings, Dolmen de Soto, Dowth, Hypogeum, Knowth, Loughcrew, Mané Lud, Mané Rutual, Newgrange, Pierres Plates, Tarxien
circles, stone *see* stone circles
cist covers 89, 121
Clear Island 28
colouring materials 91, 119, 120
construction, of megaliths 26; of tumulus at Newgrange 25
Conwell, Eugene Alfred 28
corbelling 25, 119, *6*
County Kerry, Ireland 90; *see also* Derrynablaha, Gates of Glory, Staigue Bridge
Crete, influence on passage-grave art 142
'crooks' (croziers) *see illustrations under* Mané Lud, Mané Rutual, Table des Marchands
crosses, at Cueva de Menga *80*
Cueva Belmaco 91, *124*
Cueva de Menga 30, *79, 80*
cuneiform 147

cup-and-ring art 88–91; cup marks, simple 88, 90; connected with astronomy 91

cups-and-rings, chronology 89, 90; in Argyll 88; in Italy and Spain 88, 90; meanings of 139; tools used in carving 89; *see also illustrations under* Achnabreck, Baildon Moor, Derrynablaha, Ilkley Moor, Kilmichael Glassary, Ormaig, Roughting Linn, Staigue Bridge

curvilinear, serpentiform designs 23, 27, 118–19, 121, 142; *see also illustrations under* Bryn Celli Ddu, Cueva Belmaco, Dowth, Gavrinis, Hypogeum, Ilkley Moor, Knowth, Loughcrew, Newgrange, Tarxien

Daniel, Glyn 142
Dechelette, Joseph 142
Denmark 12; *see also* Scandinavia
Derrynablaha 90, 98–100
design, sense of at Newgrange 24; in Malta 120; cup-and-ring compared to passage-grave 88–9
diffusion 140–1, 144
disc, flint 90, 142
discs in Malta 121; *see also* circles
Dolmen de Soto 30, 82–4, 85–9
dowsers 144, 149
Dowth 23, 28, 37–40
dream cult in Malta 120
drilled holes 118, 2, 5, 127–30; *see also* techniques
Druids 138, 139

Earth Mother 151; *see also* goddesses
Eday Stone 28
Egypt, pyramids 11, 12; source of civilization 143
electromagnetic forces 144, 149
Eliade, Mircea 148, 150, 151, 152
Elliot-Smith, Grafton 144

engineering of roof at Newgrange 25
England, cup-and-ring sites in 90; *see also* Avebury, Baildon Moor, Britain, Ilkley, Northumberland
entrance stones (blocking stones), at Knowth 24, 28; at Loughcrew 45; in Malta 119, 142–4; at Newgrange 23–4, 20–2
Eogan, George 26
excavations, at Knowth 27–8; in Malta 119–20

flower-like designs 23, 28; *see also illustrations under* Loughcrew
forecourts 118
Fourknocks I 28–30, 46–52
France 11, 30; circles and alignments 143; passage-grave art 23, 28–30, 140–1; statue-stelae 91; *see also* Gavrinis, Mané Lud, Mané Rutual, Menec, Pierres Plates, Roche-aux Fées, Table des Marchands
Fuente de la Zarza 91, 117–19, 120–1

Galician style of ornament 140
Gates of Glory 90
Gavrinis 23, 28–30, 144, 56–67
geomancy 149, *see also* dowsers
geometry, megalithic 143–4
Germany 121; rock art in 142
goddesses 30, 120, 140, 142, 126, 138, 139
gods, voices of 151
Göhlitzsch 142
Gozo 118, 120; map 125
Granja de Toniñuelos, La 30, 81
grave-goods 26
Graves, the Rev. Charles 90, 139
Greenwell, the Rev. William 139
gritstone, at Newgrange 24, 25

Hadingham, Evan 88, 139, 140, 145
Hagar Qim 118–19, 10, 129–31, 144

Hanging Stones 105–8; *see also* Ilkley Moor
Hart, the Rev. Mr 138
Hawkes, Terence 147
'henge' monuments 11
Herity, Michael 26, 147
hexagons 119, *see also illustrations under* Hypogeum
hidden ornament 121, 139, 36
hieroglyphics, Egyptian 148
Hill of the Witch 28, 41–43
Hitching, Francis 144
Holy of Holies 119
Hypogeum 119, 120, 126, 132–4

Iberia 140, 143; Iberian peninsula 121; *see also* Spain Portugal
ideogram 146
Ilkley Moor 90, 103–8
inscriptions, meaning of 139, 142–4; Neolithic 88
intuitive logic 147
Ireland, grave-goods 26; hidden ornament in 121; map 13; *see also* Derrynablaha, Dowth, Fourknocks, Gates of Glory, Knowth, Loughcrew, Newgrange, Staigue Bridge
Iron Age fort 139; outcrop near 97
Italy 121; carvings in Valcamonica 90–1, 142–3; *see also illustrations under* Bagnolo I, Bagnolo II, Borno, Luine, Map of Bedolina, Ossimo I
Ivimy, John 144

Jaynes, Julian 151

kerbstones 23–4, 27–8, 30; at Dowth 39; at Knowth 32–4; at Newgrange 29–31
Kerry, County of 90; *see also* Derrynablaha, Gates of Glory, Staigue Bridge
keyhole designs 89; at Ormaig 94–5; at Kilmichael Glassary 96
Kilmartin Valley 89; *see also* Argyll
Kilmichael Glassary 89–90, 96

Knockmany 28
Knowth 23, 27–30, 149, *32–8*
Kuhn, Herbert 142, 147

labyrinths 88, 139, 149, 151; at
    Bryn Celli Ddu *55*
language, in societies 148;
    Neolithic 146; structure of
    147; of symbols 121; symbols
    as 152
La Palma 91; *see also* Cueva
    Belmaco, Fuente de la Zarza,
    Roque de Teneguia
Larmor-Baden 28
La Tène art 142
Lévi-Strauss, Claude 147, 152
Lewis, Bill 144
ley lines 144
Lhwyd, Edward 138
L'Ile Longue 30
limestone, in Malta 118, 120,
    121; globigerina *131*
Loch Craignish 90, *93*
Locmariaquer 30; *see also* Mané
    Lud, Mané Rutual, Pierres
    Plates, Table des Marchands
Loughcrew 28, *41–5*
lozenges *see* diamonds
Luine *117–19*
lunar, measurement of time
    150; myths 151

Macalister, R. A. S. 139
MacWhite, Eoin 140
magic, hunting 11; sympathetic
    142; in placement of
    megaliths 149
magical analogues 148
Malta, goddesses 120, *126*, *138*,
    139; map *125*; monuments
    11, 12, 118–21; motifs 23,
    118; ornament 118–21; *see
    also* Buġibba, Ħaġar Qim,
    Hypogeum, Mnajdra,
    Sleeping Lady, Tarxien
mana (life force) 149
Mané Lud *77–8*
Mané Rutual 30, *76*
'Map of Bedolina' *110*
maps, Ireland *13*; Malta and
    Gozo *125*; Newgrange area
    17; sites mentioned in text *3*;
    sites near Carnac *18*

'map' theories 90, 139
Meath, County 23; *see also*
    Dowth, Fourknocks I,
    Knowth, Loughcrew,
    Newgrange
Mediterranean Sea 118; East
    Mediterranean 140, 143
megaliths, builders 12, 151;
    construction 25–7; dating 12;
    location 11
megalithic, building design at
    Mnajdra 118; façade 119;
    geometry 143–4
Menec, Le 9
metaphysics 147–8
Michell, John 144
Milan Museum of Archaeology
    (Borno boulder) *109*
Mnajdra 118, *2*, *127–8*
Montelius, Oscar 142
Morbihan district 30; *see also*
    Brittany
Morris, Ronald 88, 139, 143
Mother Earth 151
myths 147, 148, 150–1

National Museum, Valetta 120;
    objects from *129*, *130*, *142–6*
naturalistic designs 91, 118, 138;
    axe forms 30, 121, *109*, *111*,
    142; megalithic building 118;
    plant forms 119, *129–30*
Neolithic 11; art 142, 152;
    beliefs, mentality 141, 146,
    150–1; carvings in Italy 90;
    carvings in Malta 118;
    cemeteries 28, 89; culture 30;
    inscriptions 88; paintings 119
Newgrange 23, 30, 149;
    caretaker Michael Smith *16*;
    corbelled roof *6*; compared
    with Gavrinis 29; drawing of
    148; elevation and plan *14*;
    entrance 24, *20–2*; exterior
    19, 29–31; interior 25–6, *1*, *8*,
    24–8; map of area *17*;
    solstice at 25, *15*, *23*
Nether Largie 89, *4*
Northumberland 90, *150*

O'Kelly, Claire 25–6
O'Kelly, M. J. 23–5

oracle chamber, Hypogeum
    119, *132*
Orkney (Eday Stone) 28
Ormaig 90, *94–5*
orthostats (uprights) 24, 25, 28,
    29, 90, 118, 121, 199; *see also
    illustrations under* Dolmen de
    Soto, Dowth, Gavrinis,
    Granja de Toniñuelos, Mané
    Lud, Mané Rutual,
    Newgrange, Pierres Plates,
    Table des Marchands
Ossimo I *113*
O'Sullivan, Daniel 90, *98*

painted designs 30; cave art 11;
    in Malta 118–19, *132*, *133*
Palaeolithic art 11, 121, 142, 146
parallel lines, as symbolic 149;
    in passage-grave art 23; *see
    also illustrations under*
    Gavrinis, Loughcrew,
    Newgrange
passage-grave art 23–30, 89;
    style 88, 91, 140
passage graves 11; builders 26,
    88; *see also* Baltinglass,
    Barclodiad y Gawres, Bryn
    Celli Ddu, Clear Island,
    Cueva de Menga, Dowth,
    Dolmen de Soto, Fourknocks,
    Gavrinis, Granja de
    Toniñuelos, Knockmany,
    Knowth, Loughcrew, L'Ile
    Longue, Mané Lud, Mané
    Rutual, Newgrange, Pierres
    Plates, La Roche-aux-Fées, Le
    Rocher, Sess Kilgreen, Seefin,
    Table des Marchands
Perry, W. J. 144
Petit Mont 30
pick-dressing 24; picking 89
pictograms 146; Sumerian 147
Pierres Plates, Les 30, *68–72*
pigments 91, 119
pillar, carved 119, *129–30*
plaques, Neolithic 30, 151
Portugal 30, 140
Powell, T. G. E. 142
prehistoric art 11, 12, 90–1,
    142–3; beliefs 148–52;
    chronology 11–12, 88–9

Pythagorean theorem 143

radiocarbon dating 11–12, 140
recesses (niches, kistvaens) 25, 26
religion 142–3, 147, 151; comparative 148
Renfrew, Colin 12, 140
rings see circles, cups-and-rings, stone circles
ritual 26, 91, 118, 150–1; centres 149
Roche-aux-Fées, La 7
Rocher, Le 30
roofstone, at Newgrange 25–6
Roque de Teneguia 122–3
rosettes 90, 93, 95
Routing Linn Inscribed Rock 149

Sachsen-Anhalt, Germany 142
sacred mountain 149; objects 152; space and time 149, 150; texts 148
savage mind 147, 148
Scandinavia 11, 121, 139
Schwaller de Lubicz, R. A. 148, 153
Schwenk, Theodore 151
Scotland 88–90, 139, 143; see also Achnabreck, Argyll, Cairnbaan, Eday Stone, Kilmichael Glassary, Nether Largie, Ormaig, Temple Wood
screens, at Tarxien 120, 135, 136
Seefin 28
semiotics 147
serpentiform see curvilinear designs
Sess Kilgreen 28
Shee, Elizabeth 89
Simpson, J. Y. 150
Sleeping Lady found in Hypogeum 120, 126
Smith, Michael 16
snake patterns 142; see also curvilinear designs
solar year 150
solstices 25, 149, 150, 14, 15, 19, 23, 57
Spain 23, 140; Canary Islands 88, 91; cave painting in 11;

passage-grave art in 30; stylized symbols 142; see also Cueva Belmaco, Cueva de Menga, Dolmen de Soto, Fuente de la Zarza, Galicia, Granja de Toniñuelos, Iberia, Roque de Teneguia
spirals, at Newgrange 24–6, 138; in Canary Islands 91; in Malta 118, 119, 120, 121; in passage-grave art 23; as eyes 142; as lines of force 149–50; as path of spirit or speech 151; see also illustrations under Bagnolo II, Borno, Bugibba, Fuente de la Zarza, Haġar Qim, Knowth, Loughcrew, Newgrange, Ossimo I, Roque de Teneguia, Tarxien
Staigue Bridge 90, 97
standing stones 23, 89, 91, 143, 9, 11, 12
statue-stelae 91
stelae 88
Stone Age art 11, 90, 142; abstract symbols 12, 121, 146–8, 153; chronology 140; design 30; religion 151, 152; see also Neolithic, Palaeolithic
stone circles 11, 89, 143; Avebury 11
Stonehenge 11, 144
stones, as sacred 152; horizontal 88; types used 118; see also standing stones
Strathclyde see Argyll
structural anthropology 147
structuralism 147–8
style, cups-and-rings compared with passage-grave art 88; Breuil's categories 139; compared with Irish 30, 140; in Canary Islands 91; in Malta 119–21, 139, 140; passage-grave 27, 28
Swastika Stone 90, 103
symbols 9, 12, 23, 88, 90, 121, 142, 146, 148, 152
symbolism 146–7; abstract 12, 121, 142–3; nature of 152; in prehistoric art 12, 142

Table des Marchands 74, 75
Tara 23
Tarxien 120, 135–7, 140–7; the goddess at 151, 138, 139
Tate, George 139, 149
techniques, of carving in Ireland 89; in Italy 90–1, 142–3; in Malta 118, 120–1; of construction 26, 119
Temple Wood standing stones 12
tendril design 132
textile-like designs at Göhlitzsch 142
Thom, Alexander 91, 143–4, 149
time, Neolithic 150
tools 24, 26, 89; in Malta 118; ornaments in shape of 26
Torbhalaran 89, 90
tree of life 149
triangles 23
tumuli 23, 25, 27, 29, 30
Trigueros, Spain 30; see also Granja de Toniñuelos
trilithon 119, 127; imitation 134

Underwood, Guy 144
upright see orthostat

Valcamonica 90–1, 142–3, 109–16; see also Italy
Vico, Giambattista 147, 148
voices of the gods 151–2
von Däniken, Erich 143

Wakeman, William 138
Wales, 28; see also Barclodiad y Gawres, Bryn Celli Ddu
Watkins, Alfred 144
Wiltshire, Avebury 11, 11
writing 142, 144, 146, 147–8

Yorkshire 90; see also Baildon Moor, Ilkley Moor

Zammit, Themistocles 120
zigzag, chevron 23, 25, 26, 28, 29, 142; see also illustrations under Barclodiad y Gawres, Bryn Celli Ddu, Dolmen de Soto, Dowth, Fourknocks, Gavrinis, Loughcrew, Newgrange